HOME GUARD LIST 1941
Scottish Command

HOME GUARD LIST 1941

Scottish Command

Published from original material held by the Imperial War Museum Department of Printed Books

Published by Savannah Publications, 90 Dartmouth Road, Forest Hill, London SE23 3HZ
Tel: +44 (0) 208 244 4350 Email: savpub@dircon.co.uk
Website: www.savannah-publications.com

British Library Cataloguing in Publication Data:
A CIP catalogue record is available from the British Library

ISBN: 1 902366 25 5

Printed in the UK by Print Solutions Partnership

Cover design by Reggie Freeman

Cover photograph of the Home Guard was probably taken in the West Midlands (from the collection of Jon Mills)

INTRODUCTION

Jon Mills

Created in May 1940 when a German invasion seemed imminent, the Local Defence Volunteers (LDV) were by July - and at Winston Churchill's insistence - renamed the Home Guard (HG). In the early days there were no ranks in the force and no officers. There was a system of appointments and some of these were clearly perceived as officers, but the War Office refused to grant military status to civilians and, with it, associated powers over regular troops.

It was not until February 1941 that the Home Guard was entitled to military ranks. Following the practice of the *Army List*, all HG officers were listed in the *Home Guard List*, of which this is the first edition. A separate list was published for each of the Military Commands into which the United Kingdom was divided. Subsequent editions were published at intervals until a final 'stand down' edition, dated October 1944, but actually published in August 1945.

These are some of the most rare documents of the Second World War. The size of the Commands dictated the number of copies printed and this was usually between 300 and 500 copies per Command. With the disbandment of the Home Guard, most seem to have been destroyed. Their republication provides an opportunity to study those who formed the Home Guard and laid the basis for the efficient defence force that it became. Many of those listed had already served their country during the First World War and the frequency with which the initials DSO, MC, DCM and MM appear after the officers' names indicates many brave and experienced soldiers serving as Home Guard officers. It is also interesting to find some who had already, by the time this list was published, been rewarded for services in the Second World War. More than one holder of the George Medal, not instituted until 1940, appears in the pages of these lists.

Each list has the same format. A dated title page is followed by a listing of the units within the publication. Corresponding to the HG's operational and administrative structure, this proceeds down the chain of command from Areas, to Zones, Groups and Battalions. Battalions are numbered within the counties in the Command, with any subsidiary title indicating a town, area or sometimes public utility where the battalion is based (e.g. 35th City of London (Hackney) Bn, 52nd

County of London (Wandsworth) Gas Company Bn). Railway Company and General Post Office Battalions, together with some small independent units are also listed. At the end of each list is an alphabetical index showing on which page individuals can be found. A small section lists officers who have recently died and been removed from the List.

Within battalions, officers are listed by rank from the Commanding Officer downwards. Decorations to which they were entitled are indicated by post-nominal letters. In some cases former service is shown (for example, Major, late Rhodesia R, 2nd Lt Late E. Lanc. R.). HG battalions often varied in size and hence by number of officers. The 7th Cheshire (Crewe) Battalion has, including the regular Quartermaster (QM) and the Medical Officer, 98 officers in its ranks (including one retired Lieutenant Colonel serving as a 2nd Lieutenant). A few pages away the 11th Cheshire (Middlewich) Battalion has 38 officers (and no regular QM). The final entry for each officer gives his seniority date in the List. In the case of this List, an academic point, as they all have the date 1st February 1941, that at which HG officers were granted military rank.

These Lists will prove invaluable for medal collectors who can trace HG service and Defence Medal entitlement for many decorated officers, for local historians researching local personalities and for family historians now able, for the first time, to track down the commissioned service of their relatives who served with this unique force.

Scottish Command

From the Borders and the Lowlands to the farthest islands of the Orkneys and Shetlands, Scotland was covered by the Home Guard. Units included such oddities as mobile companies raised from students of the Senior Training Corps at Edinburgh University. Scotland's main industrial city, Glasgow, was heavily raided, leading to the award of one of only thirteen George Medals (GM) to the Home Guard. Captain A.R. Ballantyne, 2nd Dumbartonshire Battalion had already had his GM announced in the *London Gazette* by the time this *List* was published but it obviously missed the copy deadline for inclusion. Serving with the Singer Factory Home Guard on Clydebank, Captain Ballantyne had on two consecutive nights in March 1941 saved lives and property during air raids.

During training many Home Guard units seem to have had accidents with grenades. Out of a total of 137 awards to the Home Guard, 25 were for saving life as a result of grenade accidents. One of these was still three years away for Lieutenant T.F. Wilson, 1st Fifeshire Battalion who was to sustain severe injuries and be awarded an MBE in 1944.

As in most areas, officers in the Scottish Home Guard came from a variety of military backgrounds. The Commanding Officer of the 1st Zetland (the official title of the Shetland Islands) Battalion, was a Knight and a retired Lieutenant RNVR. In the 1st Kirkcudbrightshire Battalion, the Commanding Officer was a retired Brigadier General, as was one of the Company Commanders. Other officers included a retired Colonel with a DSO serving as a Captain, two former officers of the Canadian Army and a peer of the realm with former service in the Royal Scots Greys, serving as a Lieutenant. Many similar stories may be discovered in this *List*.

Jon Mills

TABLE OF CONTENTS

TABLE OF CONTENTS - continued

BATTALIONS - continued

ARMY COUNCIL

CAPTAIN the Right Honourable H. DAVID R. MARGESSON, M.C., M.P., ret.
SECRETARY OF STATE FOR WAR
(President of the Army Council.)

BRIGADIER-GENERAL the Lord CROFT, C.M.G., T.D., ret. T.A.
PARLIAMENTARY UNDER-SECRETARY OF STATE FOR WAR
(Vice President of the Army Council.)

GENERAL Sir JOHN G. DILL, K.C.B., C.M.G., D.S.O., Col. E. Lan. R., i.d.c., p.s.c.†
A.D.C.
CHIEF OF THE IMPERIAL GENERAL STAFF (First Military Member.)

LIEUTENANT-GENERAL Sir RONALD F. ADAM, Bt., C.B., D.S.O., O.B.E., Col. Comdt.
R.A. and A.E.C., i.d.c., p.s.c.†
ADJUTANT-GENERAL TO THE FORCES (Second Military Member.)

GENERAL Sir WALTER K. VENNING, K.C.B., C.M.G., C.B.E., M.C., Col. D.C.L.I., p.s.c.†
QUARTER-MASTER-GENERAL TO THE FORCES (Third Military Member.)

LIEUTENANT-GENERAL (temp.) Sir HENRY R. POWNALL, K.B.E., C.B., D.S.O., M.C., i.d.c.,
p.s.c.†
VICE-CHIEF OF THE IMPERIAL GENERAL STAFF (Fourth Military Member.)

LIEUTENANT-COLONEL Sir EDWARD W. M. GRIGG, K.C.M.G., K.C.V.O., D.S.O., M.C., M.P., ret.
PARLIAMENTARY UNDER-SECRETARY OF STATE FOR WAR (Civil Member.)

CAPTAIN E. D. SANDYS, M.P., R.A. (T.A.)
FINANCIAL SECRETARY OF THE WAR OFFICE (Finance Member.)

Sir ROBERT J. SINCLAIR, K.B.E.
DIRECTOR-GENERAL OF ARMY REQUIREMENTS.

Sir JAMES GRIGG, K.C.B., K.C.S.I.
PERMANENT UNDER-SECRETARY OF STATE FOR WAR
(Secretary of the Army Council.)

56455-3(5)

HOME GUARD DIRECTORATE

Director–General	Maj.-Gen. (actg. 3/6/41) the Visct. Bridgeman, D.S.O., M.C., ret. pay (Res. of Off.) p.s.c.✝ (L)	3/ 6/41
Military Assistant	Capt. (actg. 4/3/41) L. A. Impey, Gen. List	3/ 6/41
Deputy Director	Lt.-Col. (temp. 18/11/40) K. Bayley, O.B.E., Oxf. & Bucks. L.I., p.s.c.✝	–
Inspector of Administration	Lt.-Col. (actg. 7/5/41) P. C. Vellacott, D.S.O., Gen. List	7/ 5/41
Dep. Asst. Directors	Maj. (temp. 27/6/41) U. O. V. Verney, ret. pay (Res. of Off.)	27/ 3/41
	Capt. A. M Lindsay-Thomson, Res. of Off.	–
Staff Captains	Capt. (temp. 1/3/41) E. H. Ryley, Gen. List	30/11/40
	Capt. (temp. 26/2/40) C. E. Hodgson, M.B.E., R. War. R.	3/12/40
	Capt. R. T. Burton, O.B.E., Res. of Off.	–
	Capt. T. R. Wilbraham, Rifle Bde.	21/ 5/41

TERRITORIAL ARMY

Director–General	Maj.-Gen. (actg. 3/6/41) the Visct. Bridgeman, D.S.O., M.C. ret. pay (Res. of Off.) p.s.c.✝ (L)	–
Deputy Director–General	Lt.-Col. J. A. Longmore, M.B.E., T.D., Herts. R. (T.A.) t.a.	–

56455-3(6)

SPECIAL APPOINTMENTS

POST OFFICE GROUP

Commander	Reid, Col. F., M.C., T.D. (Lt. Col. ret. T.A.)	1/ 2/41
Second in command	Edwards, Lt.-Col. L. J.	1/ 2/41

_____

LONDON MIDLAND AND SCOTTISH RAILWAY GROUP

Commander	Hussey, Col. G.S., M.C. (Capt. late R.E.)	1/ 2/41

_____

SOUTHERN RAILWAY GROUP

Commander	Wymer, Col. F. J. (Capt. late R.G.A.)	1/ 2/41
Staff Officers	Ellson, Lt.-Col. K. R. (Lt. T.A.Res.)	1/ 2/41
	Layton, Lt.-Col. H. F., M.C. (Capt. late Rifle Bde.)	1/ 2/41
Staff Officer (A)	Mathews, Maj. H. S.	1/ 2/41
Assistant Staff Officer (A)	Cooper, Capt. C. J.	1/ 2/41
Assistant Staff Officer (G)	Reynolds, Lt. C. H.	1/ 2/41
Signals Officer	Hall, Maj. G. L.	1/ 2/41
Transport Officer	Potter, Maj. A. B.	1/ 8/41

SCOTTISH COMMAND

| General Staff Officer, 1st grade | Hutchison, Lt.-Col. (actg. 13/3/41) J. R. H., T.D., ret., t.a. | 13/ 3/4 |

General Staff Officer, 1st grade   Hutchison, Lt.-Col. (actg. 13/3/41)
     J. R. H., T.D., ret., t.a.   13/ 3/4

General Staff Officer, 3rd grade   Turcan, Capt. H. H., 1 Fife and
     Forfar Yeo.   17/ 4/4

Dep. Asst. Adjt. & Qr.-Mr.-Gen.   Little, Maj. (actg. 20/8/40)
     W. J. H., R.War.R.   13/ 3/4

Special Appointment   Wiles, Capt. E.   1/ 7/4

NORTH HIGHLAND AREA

Commander   Usher, Col. (temp. 11/10/40) C. M.,
     D.S.O., O.B.E., Gordons (1)   29/ 6/4

NO.1 ZONE

Commander   Bulloch, Col. R. A., D.S.O. (Col.
     ret. pay)   1/ 2/4

Second-in-Command   Mackenzie, Lt.-Col. D. W. A. D.,
     C.V.O., D.S.O. (Maj. ret. pay)   1/ 2/4

Territorial Army Association ⎫   County of Inverness T.A. Association,
administering   ⎬   57, Church Street, Inverness.
    ⎭

INVERNESS GROUP

Commander   Cameron of Lochiel, Col. Sir
     Donald W., K.T., C.M.G., A.D.C.,
     ret. Mila.   1/ 2/41

Staff Officer   Gibson, Capt. M.   1/ 2/41

INVERNESS GROUP

1st INVERNESS-SHIRE (EAST & NAIRNSHIRE) BATTALION

Lt.-Colonel
Marshall, F. J., C.B., C.M.G., D.S.O. (Maj.-Gen. ret. pay)   1/ 2/41

Majors
Allardyce, J. G. B., C.M.G., D.S.O. (Col. ret. pay)   1/ 2/41
Leven & Melville, The Earl of, K.T. (Bt.-Col. late T.A.)   1/ 2/41
Fraser, Hon. A., D.S.O. (Lt.-Col. late T.A.)   1/ 2/41
Ross, J. A., T.D. (Maj. late R.A.)   1/ 2/41
Grant, J. P., M.C., T.D. (Bt.Col. late T.A.)   1/ 2/41

Captains
Drake, J. H., O.B.E., M.C. (Maj. late T.A.)   1/ 2/41
MacKay, W. (Capt. late Camerons) 1/ 2/41
Fraser, H. F., C.M.G., D.S.O. (Col. ret. pay)   1/ 2/41
Wallace, R. F. H., C.M.G. (Col. ret. pay)   1/ 2/41

Lieutenants
Will, R. R., C.I.E., D.S.O. V.D., (Lt.-Col. R.A. T.A.)   1/ 2/41
Fraser, D. M., M.C. (Capt. late R.E.)   1/ 2/41
Kemble, H. L., M.V.O. (Capt. late S. G'ds.)   1/ 2/41
Stewart, G. (Lt. late Ind.Army) 1/ 2/41
Vince, A. H. (Capt. late W.I.R.)   1/ 2/41
McIntosh, M. (Capt. late T.A.) 1/ 2/41
Gram, P. M., D.S.O. (Lt.-Col. late Camerons)   1/ 2/41
Cameron, A. (Maj. late Camerons)   1/ 2/41
Stuart, R., M.B.E.   1/ 2/41
Webb, T. L. (Capt. late Green Howards)   1/ 2/41
Mackintosh, J. (Lt. late Camerons)   1/ 2/41

Lieutenants - contd.
Macvinish, J. A. (2/Lt. late Camerons)   1/ 2/41
Hill, J. B. (Capt. late R.F.A.) 1/ 2/41
White, T. D.   1/ 2/41
Baillie, D. G., C.M.G., D.S.O., T.D. (Col. late T.A.)   1/ 2/41
Allanby, R. H. (Maj. late Seaforth)   1/ 2/41
Gourlay, A.   1/ 2/41
Forbes, G. C.   1/ 8/41
Hone, R. C. (Capt. late R.E.) 1/ 8/41
Noble, D. (Lt. late Camerons) 1/ 8/41

2nd Lieutenants
Donald, R., M.B.E., (Capt. late R.A.F.)   1/ 2/41
Fraser, D., D.S.O., M.C., T.D., (Maj. late R.H.A.)   1/ 2/41
Macleod, A., (Capt. late R.E.) 1/ 2/41
Boag, J.   1/ 2/41
Taylor, A.   1/ 2/41
MacGillivray, C. F. (Capt. late Camerons)   1/ 2/41
Mackenzie, D. Mc L.   1/ 2/41
Stewart, R. H.   1/ 2/41
Gillespie, G. M.   1/ 2/41
Watson, A. J.   1/ 2/41
Clarke, A. C. K. S., (Maj. late Ind. Army)   1/ 2/41
Swann, W. M.   1/ 2/41
Macgillivray, J. F.   1/ 2/41
Walker, T. B., M.C., (Lt. late H.L.I.)   1/ 6/41

Adjutant & Quarter-Master
Brinckman, Capt. Sir Theodore E. W., Bt., (Res. of Off.)   1/10/40

Medical Officer
Mills, Maj. E., M.B.   1/ 2/41

2nd INVERNESS-SHIRE (WEST) BATTALION

Lt.-Colonel
Sopper, F. W. (Lt.-Col. ret. pay)   1/ 2/41

Majors
Laughton, F. E., M.C., T.D., (Col. T.A. Gen. List)   1/ 2/41
Fell, Sir Godfrey B. H., K.C.I.E., C.S.I.   1/ 2/41
Walker, J. D. G., D.S.O., O.B.E., (Lt.-Col. late R.E.)   1/ 2/41

Captains
Biggs, L., (Lt. late R.N.V.R.)   1/ 2/41
Macdonald, A. K.   1/ 2/41
Mackenzie, E. M. C., O.B.E. (Capt. late R. Mar.)   1/ 2/41
Macdonald, J. A. R., (Capt. late R.A.S.C.)   1/ 2/41
Mackenzie, F. S.   1/ 2/41
Mills, D., (Maj. late Hampshire R.)   1/ 2/41
Shairp, W., M.C. (Capt. late A. & S.H.)   1/ 7/41

Lieutenants
Reid-Thomas, D. D.   1/ 2/41
Weston, S. H.   1/ 2/41
Macleod-Carey, M., (Capt. late T.A.)   1/ 2/41
Donald, D. A., (Lt. late T.A.)   1/ 2/41
Finlayson, D.   1/ 2/41
Graham, M. A.   1/ 2/41
Maccullum, H.   1/ 2/41
Whyte, F., M.C., (Lt. late R.G.A.)   1/ 2/41
Cameron-Head, F. S. (Lt. late T.A.)   1/ 2/41

Lieutenants - contd.
Abinger, The Lord, D.S.O., (Lt.-Col. late R.A.)   1/ 2/41
Duthie, J.   28/ 7/41

2nd Lieutenants
Sutherland, J. R. S., (Capt. late R.E.)   1/ 2/41
Bradley, F. W.   1/ 2/41
Cotton, M. B.   1/ 2/41
Parfitt, A. H.   1/ 2/41
Grant, E.   1/ 2/41
Macleod, I.   1/ 2/41
Maccallum, J.   1/ 2/41
Reilly, J.   1/ 2/41
Macleod, N.   1/ 2/41
Maccoll, C.   1/ 2/41
Paterson, W. A.   1/ 2/41
McGorum, J. A.   1/ 2/41
McDonnell, H. C.   1/ 2/41
Gray, J., M.C., T.D., (Maj. late R. Scots)   1/ 2/41
Downie, D. C.   1/ 2/41
Ramsden, B. P. (2/Et. late 5th Innis. D.G.)   1/ 2/41

Adjutant & Quarter-Master
Davidson, Capt. D. G., ret. pay   1/ 2/41

Medical Officer
Wilson, Maj. W. D., M.B.   1/ 2/41

NORTH HIGHLAND AREA - contd.

NO.1 ZONE - contd.

NORTHERN GROUP

| Commander | Romanes, Col. J. G. P., D.S.O. | |
| | (Col. ret. pay) (Res. of Off.) | †/ 2/41 |

1st CAITHNESS BATTALION

Lt.-Colonel			Lieutenants - contd.	
McHardy, I., (Capt. ret.)	1/ 2/41		Barnetson, J. (Lt. late	
			Seaforth)	1/ 2/41
			Miller, W.	1/ 6/41

Majors		
Reid, W. (Capt. late Seaforth)	1/ 2/41	
Mackenzie, D. M., (Lt. late		2nd Lieutenants
R. Scots)	1/ 2/41	Matheson, G.	1/ 2/41
		Shearer, D. F.	1/ 2/41

| Captain | | |
| Mackay, J. T. | 1/ 2/41 | Adjutant & Quarter-Master |

Lieutenants			Medical Officer	
Campbell, S.	1/ 2/41		Mackay, Maj. R. H., M.B.	1/ 2/41
Simpson, D. R.	1/ 2/41			
MacInnis, J. (Lt. late				
Camerons)	1/ 2/41			
Bremner, J.	1/ 2/41			
Mowat, R. B.	1/ 2/41			
Younger, J.	1/ 2/41			
Lewis, D. G.				

NORTH HIGHLAND AREA - contd.

NO.1 ZONE - contd.

NORTHERN GROUP - contd

1st SUTHERLAND BATTALION

Lt.-Colonel
Sutherland, The Duke of,
K.T., P.C. (Hon..Coll.T.A.) 1/ 2/41

Majors
Chaplin, The Visct., (Maj.
late T.A.)   1/ 2/41
Priestley, W. (Maj. late
R.F.A.)   1/ 2/41
Campbell, I. M. (Capt. late
R.G.A.)   1/ 2/41
Sutherland, D. (Capt. late
Seaforth)   1/ 2/41
Hartley, J. C., D.S.O.,
(Lt.-Col. late R. Fus.)   1/ 2/41
Cuthbert, J. M., (Maj. late
R.A.M.C.)   1/ 2/41

Captains
Sinclair, R. F., T.D. (Maj.
late Seaforth)   1/ 2/41
Grant, R., (Capt. late T.A.)   1/ 2/41
Macrae, D. L., (Capt. late
T.A.)   1/ 2/41
Edwards-Moss, J. (Maj. late
R.G.A.)   1/ 2/41

Lieutenants
Macrae, D. K.   1/ 2/41
Mackay, J. S., (Lt. ret.)   1/ 2/41
Brannen, E. W., M.M.   1/ 2/41
Mackintosh, J.   1/ 2/41
Ross, R., (Lt. late Seaforth)   1/ 2/41

Lieutenants - contd.
Macintosh, H. (Lt. late
Seaforth)   1/ 2/41
Mackay, A. W.   1/ 2/41
Grant, W. W.   1/ 2/41
Fraser, J. M.   1/ 2/41
Elliott, M.   1/ 2/41
Hames, W. M. (Capt. late R.E.)   1/ 2/41
VC Forbes-Robertson, J., D.S.O.,
M.C., (Col. ret. pay)(Res.
of Off.)   1/ 2/41
Wigan, Sir Roderick G., Bt.,
(Lt. late R.A.S.C.)   1/ 2/41

2nd Lieutenants
Grant, R.   1/ 2/41
Ross, H. A.   1/ 2/41
Mackay, R.   1/ 2/41
Sinclair, G. J.   1/ 2/41
Urquhart, W. B.   1/ 2/41
Munro, H.   1/ 2/41
Haig-Thomas, P.   24/ 7/41

Adjutant & Quarter-Master

Medical Officer
Watson, Maj. J. M.D.   1/ 2/41

1st ROSS-SHIRE BATTALION

Lt.-Colonel
Dick-Lauder, Sir John N. D.,
Bt. (Lt.-Col. ret. Ind. Army) 1/ 2/41

Majors
Mackenzie, Sir Hector, Bt.,
M.C., (Capt. late T.A.)   1/ 2/41
Prickett, C. B., (Rear
Admiral ret.)   1/ 2/41
Smith, A. E. D., (Maj. late
R.F.A.)   1/ 2/41
Doran, C. C. H., (Maj. late
R.E.)   1/ 2/41
Bannerman, W. G.   1/ 2/41
Matheson, Sir Torquhil G.,
K.C.B., C.M.G., (Gen. ret.
pay)   1/ 2/41

Captains
Maclennan, J.   1/ 2/41
Geekie, D., (Capt. late
Sco. Rif.)   1/ 2/41
Anderson, R. T. W. W.   1/ 2/41
Seth-Smith, H. K., (Lt. late
Midd'x. R.)   1/ 2/41

Lieutenants
Ross, T. D.   1/ 2/41
Gordon, G. A., (Capt. late
R.A.S.C.)   1/ 2/41
Gill, W. H. M.   1/ 2/41
Conyngham, The Marq., (late
R. Inniskilling Fus.)   1/ 2/41
Gilchrist, H.   1/ 2/41
MacLennan, J., (Lt. late
T.A.)   1/ 2/41
Noble, H. C., (Lt. late
R.E.)   1/ 2/41
Ross, G.   1/ 2/41
Cameron, I. L.   1/ 2/41
Forsyth, G.   1/ 2/41
Gordon, A. A., (Lt. late
Seaforth)   1/ 2/41
Maclean, R., (Capt. late
R.F.A.)   1/ 2/41
Smith, W. G.   1/ 2/41
MacLennan, D.   1/ 2/41

Lieutenants - contd.
Scott, A.   1/ 2/41
Mackenzie, M.   1/ 2/41
Mackenzie, A., D.C.M.   1/ 2/41
Murchison, J. A.   1/ 2/41
Portman, Hon. Gerald B.,
(Capt. ret.)   1/ 2/41
Badger, T. R., O.B.E.,
(Lt.-Col. ret. pay)   1/ 2/41
Gordon, J. O., (Capt. late
Seaforth)   1/ 2/41
Ross, D.   1/ 2/41
Budge, D., (Lt. late
Camerons)   1/ 2/41
Murray, J., (Lt. late K.O.S.B.) 1/ 2/41
Urquhart, D. I., (Capt. late
Ind. Army)   1/ 2/41
Powrie, C. F.   1/ 2/41
D. J. Matheson   24/ 6/41

2nd Lieutenants
Campbell-Crawford, A.,
(Sub. Lt. late R.N.V.R.)   1/ 2/41
Mackenzie, R., D.C.M., M.M.   1/ 2/41
Grant, D. D.   1/ 2/41
Houston, J., (Lt. late
Camerons)   1/ 2/41
Thomson, J. S.   1/ 2/41
Fowler, A., (Capt. late R.G.A.) 1/ 2/41
Ross, G., M.M.   1/ 2/41
Macrae, W.   1/ 2/41
Macleod, N.   1/ 2/41
Douglas, G.   1/ 2/41
Macdonald, R. R. M., (Capt.
late Seaforth)   1/ 2/41
Matheson, H. I.   1/ 6/41

Adjutant & Quarter-Master
McIver, Capt. (actg. 1/3/41) E.,
Gen. List Inf.   1/ 3/41

Medical Officer
Mackenzie, Maj. C., M.B.,   1/ 2/41

NORTH HIGHLAND AREA - contd.

NO.1 ZONE - contd.

NORTHERN GROUP - contd.

1st LEWIS BATTALION

Lt.-Colonel
Macsween, J., (Capt. late Spec. List)　　　1/ 2/41

Majors
Macrae, M.　　　1/ 2/41
Mackay, J., (Lt. late King's Own R.)　　　1/ 2/41
Mackay, D.　　　1/ 2/41
Mackenzie, C. S.　　　1/ 2/41
Carmichael, I., D.S.O., M.C., (Maj. late P. Corps)　　　1/ 7/41

Captains
Maclean, M. M., M.C., (2/Lt. late R.F.A.)　　　1/ 2/41
Macneill, D., (Capt. late R. Fus.)　　　1/ 2/41
Murray, D.　　　1/ 2/41

Lieutenants
Campbell, W.　　　1/ 2/41
Matheson, A., (Lt. late R.A.)　　　1/ 2/41
Maclean, G. D.　　　1/ 2/41
Marcarthur, D. W., (Lt. late R.A.)　　　1/ 2/41
Mackinnon, D.　　　1/ 2/41
Smith, K.　　　1/ 2/41
Macarthur, J.　　　1/ 2/41
Mackay, J.　　　1/ 2/41
Smith, J.　　　1/ 2/41
Macleod, A.　　　1/ 2/41
Morrison, J.　　　1/ 2/41
Ferguson, D.　　　1/ 2/41
Macleod, M.　　　1/ 2/41

Lieutenants - contd.
Smith, D.　　　1/ 2/41
Morrison, D.　　　1/ 2/41
Macleod, M.　　　1/ 2/41
Baker, T., D.C.M.　　　1/ 2/41
Macdonald, T. C., (Lt. ret. R.N.)　　　1/ 2/41
Mitchell, J., (2/Lt. late M.C.)　　　1/ 2/41
Pirie, T. S.　　　1/ 2/41
Mackenzie, A. J., D.S.C.　　　1/ 2/41
Scoular, J. D.　　　1/ 2/41

2nd Lieutenants
Maclean, A. J.　　　1/ 2/41
Mackenzie, R.　　　1/ 2/41
Skinner, P. W. G.　　　1/ 2/41
Morrison, R.　　　1/ 2/41
Macarthur, D.　　　1/ 2/41

Adjutant & Quarter-Master

Medical Officer
McCleod, Maj. C. B., M.B., (Maj. late R.A.M.C.)　　　1/ 2/41

NORTH HIGHLAND AREA - contd.

NO.2 ZONE (ELGIN)

Commander	Macdonald, Col., A. D., T.D. (Bt. Col. ret. T.A.)	1/ 2/41
Assistant to Zone Commander	Allan, Maj. W. D., (Lt.-Col. late Black Watch)	1/ 2/41
	White, Capt. R. H., M.B.E. (Capt. late Seaforth)	1/ 2/41
Zone Liaison Officer	Moray, Capt., The Earl of, M.C., (Capt. late R.A.F.)	1/ 2/41
Zone Chief Guide	Stuart, Capt. M. G.	1/ 2/41
Territorial Army Associations administering		
Moray Battalion	County of Moray T.A. Association, 7, North Street, Elgin.	
Banff Battalion	County of Banff T.A. Association, 17, Fife Street, Dufftown.	

1st MORAYSHIRE BATTALION

Lt.-Colonel

Hopkinson, J. O., D.S.O., M.C., (Lt.-Col. late Seaforth) 1/ 2/41

Majors

Baird, Sir H. B. Douglas, K.C.B., C.M.G., C.I.E., D.S.O., (Gen. ret. Ind. Army) (Col. S. Lan. R.)	1/ 2/41
Petrie, J. N.	1/ 2/41
Macdonald, A. H., M.C. (Capt. late Seaforth)	1/ 2/41
Dunbar, J. B., (Lt.-Col. late Camerons)	1/ 2/41
Hendry, F. C., O.B.E., M.C., (Capt. late T.A.)	1/ 2/41

Captains

Cooper, H. R., (Capt. late Ind. Army)	1/ 2/41
Scott, Sir R. Russell, K.C.B., C.S.I., I.S.O.	1/ 2/41
Petrie, W. R., (Capt. late Seaforth)	1/ 2/41
Hunter, T., (Lt. late H.L.I.)	1/ 2/41

Lieutenants

McColl, C. A.	1/ 2/41
Fraser, W., D.C.M.	1/ 2/41
Ogston, T., (2/Lt. late Seaforth)	1/ 2/41
Forsyth, R. K., (Capt. late Seaforth)	1/ 2/41
Peever, R.	1/ 2/41
McCallum, H.	1/ 2/41
Roger, J. L.	1/ 2/41
Stratton, W., (Lt. late T.A.)	1/ 2/41

56455-3(15)

NORTH HIGHLAND AREA - contd.

No. 2 ZONE (ELGIN) - contd.

1st Morayshire.Battalion - contd.

Lieutenants - contd.
Lofting, R. C. J., (Maj. late
R.I.C.)   1/ 2/41
Mustard, W. S., (Lt. late
Seaforth)   1/ 2/41
Grant, R. I. D.   1/ 2/41
Coupland, W.   1/ 2/41
Wilson, R.   1/ 2/41
Davies, H. M., D.S.C.,
(Brig.-Gen. ret. pay)   1/ 2/41
Hamilton-Grierson, P. F., M.B.E.
(Capt. late R.S. Fus.)   1/ 2/41
McIntosh, C., M.M.   1/ 2/41
Cochrane, L. C.   1/ 2/41
Jefferson, J., D.C.M.,
(Capt. late Gordons)   1/ 2/41
Reid, J.   1/ 2/41
Heir, J. (Lt. late
Cameronians)   29/ 5/41
Latham, J. S.   19/ 6/41
Benson, W. T., (Surgeon Lt.
late R.N.).   19/ 6/41
Selbie, J. S. (Capt. late
R.S.F.)   27/ 6/41
Kellett, J. T.   18/ 7/41

2nd Lieutenants
Stephen, W. M.   1/ 2/41
Paterson, T., (Lt. late
Seaforth)   1/ 2/41
Simpson, C. L.   1/ 2/41
Fraser, J. C.   1/ 2/41
Young, W. J.   1/ 2/41
Manson, T.   1/ 2/41
Keith, C.   1/ 2/41
Buchan, W., M.M.   1/ 2/41
Lamond, J.   1/ 2/41
McIntosh, D.   1/ 2/41
Morren, J.   1/ 2/41
Mitchell, A. H.   1/ 2/41
Grant, R. D. G.   1/ 2/41
Grierson, C.   1/ 2/41
Ferguson, R. A.   29/ 5/41
Rose, W. G. A.   17/ 6/41
Brown, G. R.   29/ 5/41
Findlay, G., D.C.M.   18/ 7/41

Adjutant & Quarter-Master
Macmillan, Capt. (actg. 1/3/41)
D. M., Gen. List Inf.   10/ 4/41

Medical Officer
Collis, Maj. E. L., C.B.E.   1/ 2/41

1st BANFFSHIRE BATTALION

Lt.-Colonel
Burn, H. P., C.M.G., D.S.O.
(Hon. Brig.-Gen. ret. pay)   1/ 2/41

Majors
Noble, D., M.C.. (Capt.
late Seaforth)   1/ 2/41
Walker, W. R., (Capt. late
Border)   1/ 2/41
Bain, L., (Capt. late Gordons)   1/ 2/41
McHaffie, W. J., (Capt. late
K.O.S.B.)   1/ 2/41
Fowlie, S. S., M.C.,
(Capt. late Seaforth)   1/ 2/41
Munro, J. H., M.C., (Capt. late
Seaforth)   1/ 2/41

Captains
Wood, J., M.C., (Maj. late
Manch. R.)   1/ 2/41
Chisholm, D.   1/ 2/41
Ricketts, R. B., (Capt. late R.A.)1/ 2/41
Young, J. E., (Capt. late
R.A.S.C.)   28/ 7/41

Lieutenants
Findlater, A. J.   1/ 2/41
McHardy, A. S.   1/ 2/41
Goodall, G. F.   1/ 2/41
Thomson, F. C.   1/ 2/41
Kemp, W. G.   1/ 2/41
Milton, J. S.   1/ 2/41
Coull, C. G., (Lt. late R.N.R.)   1/ 2/41
Hutchinson, T. E.   1/ 2/41
Hoggan, W. M., (Capt. late
Suffolk R.)   1/ 2/41
Esslemont, E.   1/ 2/41
Oswald, C. G.   1/ 2/41
Grant, T.   1/ 2/41
McNiven, D.   1/ 2/41
Robertson, H.   1/ 2/41
Newlands, R., M.M.   1/ 2/41
Allan, R.   1/ 2/41
McGregor, W. G.   1/ 2/41
McGregor, J. A.   1/ 2/41
Borrell, M. T.   1/ 2/41
Newlands, F.   1/ 2/41
Watt, G.   1/ 2/41
Stuart, W. D.   28/ 7/41

2nd Lieutenant
McDonald, D.   28/ 7/41

Adjutant & Quarter-Master

Medical Officer
Paterson, Maj. A. S., M.B.   1/ 2/41

NORTH HIGHLAND AREA

No. 3 ZONE (ABERDEEN)

Commander	Brooke, Col. A. (Maj. late Ind. Army)	1/ 2/41
Staff Officer (A) & (Q)	Milne, Capt. J. N.	1/ 2/41
Zone Liaison Officer	Black, Capt. A. (Lt. late R.E.)	1/ 2/41
Territorial Army Association administering	Aberdeen T.A. Association, 5, East Craibstone Street, Aberdeen.	

1st ABERDEENSHIRE (BUCHAN) BATTALION

Lt.-Colonel

Burnett-Stuart, Sir John T., G.C.B., K.B.E., C.M.G., D.S.O. (Gen. ret. pay) (Res. of Off.)	1/ 2/41

Majors

Littlejohn, W. M. (Lt.-Col. late T.A.)	1/ 2/41
Smith, J. A., M.C. (Lt. late London Scottish)	1/ 2/41
Fraser, C., M.C. (Capt. late Manch. R.)	1/ 2/41
Grant, J. S.	1/ 2/41
Bruce, W. M. (Lt. late Gordons)	1/ 2/41
Ross, D. (Capt. late Seaforths)	1/ 2/41

Captains

Duncan, G., (Lt. late Gordons)	1/ 2/41
Troup, A. D.	1/ 2/41
Kilgour, J. F.	1/ 2/41
Duncan, A. T.	1/ 2/41
Saltoun, The Lord, M.C., (Maj. late Gordons)	1/ 2/41

Lieutenants

Morrison, J.G., M.C. (Lt. late Worcs. Regt.)	1/ 2/41
Mitchell, J.	1/ 2/41
Buchan, J. I., D.S.O. (Capt. late Black Watch)	1/ 2/41
Lownie, J. M.	1/ 2/41
Joss, W.	1/ 2/41
Barclay, J.	1/ 2/41
McWillie, J.	1/ 2/41
Johnston, R. H.	1/ 2/41
McLeman, J.	1/ 2/41
Simpson, J. S.	1/ 2/41
Greig, W. A.	1/ 2/41
Philip, R.	1/ 2/41
Symon, J. W.	1/ 2/41
Grant, H. M.	1/ 2/41
Taylor, A. E. M. (2/Lt. late Gordons)	1/ 2/41

56455-3(17)

Lieutenants - contd.

Dinnes, G. H., M.M.	1/ 2/41
Anderson, A.	1/ 2/41
Mitchell, G. H. (Capt. late Gordons)	1/ 2/41
Duthie, E.	1/ 2/41
Taggart, G. J.	1/ 2/41
Gilson, C. H.	1/ 2/41
Buchanan, T. A.	1/ 7/41

2nd Lieutenants

Glennie, C.	1/ 2/41
Cumming, G. M.	1/ 2/41
Barclay, A.	1/ 2/41
Shewan, W. M.	1/ 2/41
Ironside, J. W.	1/ 2/41
Rennie, G. A.	1/ 2/41
Watson, G. S.	1/ 2/41
Morrice, I. R. C.	1/ 2/41
Godfrey, E. T. H., (2/Lt. late R.G.A.)	1/ 2/41
Davis, F. W.	1/ 2/41

Adjutant & Quarter-Master

Ledingham, Capt. J., T.D., Gordons	1/ 2/41

Medical Officer

Leith, Maj. J. W., M.B.	1/ 2/41

2nd ABERDEENSHIRE (CENTRAL) BATTALION

Lt.-Colonel
Yates, R. J. B., D.S.O., (Col.
ret. Ind. Army)   1/ 2/41

Majors
Spence, H. R. (Capt. late
R.A.F.)   1/ 2/41
Ogilvy, D., C.I.E., D.S.O.,
O.B.E., (Hon. Brig. ret. pay) 1/ 2/41
Davidson, T. D.S.O., T.D.,
(Col. late T.A.)   1/ 2/41
Lyall, W., M.C., T.D.,
(Maj. late Gordons)   1/2/41
Cook, J. M. (Maj. late Gordons) 17/ 6/41

Captains
Farquharson, W.   1/ 2/41
Dean, W. (Capt. late R.E.)   1/ 2/41
White, J. S. M. (2/Lt. late
M.G.Corps.)   17/ 6/41

Lieutenants
Watt, J.   1/ 2/41
Watt, A. S. (Capt. late R.Scots.) 1/ 2/41
Ingleby, J. A.   1/ 2/41
Cruickshank, R. W. (Lt. late
Malayan Infy.)   1/ 2/41
Mackie, B.   1/ 2/41
Forbes, The Lord (Maj. late
G. Gds.)   1/ 2/41

56455-3(18)

Lieutenants — contd.
Ellis, W.   1/ 2/41
Wishart, J. M.   1/ 2/41
Fraser, K.   1/ 2/41
Burnett, A. M. (Capt. late
K.A. Rif.)   1/ 2/41
Crichton, A., T.D., (Maj. T.A.) 1/ 2/41
Dean, J. B.   1/ 2/41
Haughton, W. T. H.   1/ 2/41
Smith, A.   1/ 2/41
Stuart, G. C.   1/ 2/41
Maitland, G. R.   17/ 6/41

2nd Lieutenants
Mitchell, J. S. (Lt. late R.A.)   1/ 2/41
Kellas, J. (Capt. late Gordons)   1/ 2/41
Gall, J. R.   1/ 2/41
Rose, W. G.   1/ 2/41
Watson, W.   15/ 7/41

Adjutant & Quarter-Master
Mills, Capt. J. E. (ret.
Ind. Army)   10/ 2/41

Medical Officer
Orr, Maj. Sir John B., Kt., D.S.O.,
M.C., M.D. (Maj. late R.A.M.C.) 1/ 2/41

3rd ABERDEENSHIRE (SOUTH & KINCARDINE-SHIRE) BATTALION

Lt.-Colonel

Burnett of Leys, Sir James
L. G., Bt., C.B., C.M.G., D.S.O.
(Maj. Gen. ret. pay)(Res. of
Off.)   1/ 2/41

Majors

Caldwell, K. F. T. (Capt.
late R.F.A.)   1/ 2/41
Mackenzie, Sir Victor A. F.
D.S.O., M.V.O. (Col. Res.
of Off.)   1/ 2/41
Cowell-Smith, R. (Maj. late R.A.) 1/ 2/41
Miller, J. (Lt. late R.E.)   1/ 2/41
Borthwick, E. K. D.S.O., M.C.
(Capt. late K.A. Rif.)   1/ 2/41
Christie, G. S. (Maj. late
R.T.C.)   1/ 2/41
Burness, J. (Flt./Cmdr. late
R.A.F.)   1/ 2/41

Captains

Russell, W. M. (Lt. late Gordons) 1/ 2/41
Mutch, A. R. T.D., (Maj.
late R.A.)   1/ 2/41
Knox, A. C.   1/ 2/41
McLean, G. N. (Maj. late
Gordons)   1/ 2/41
Ross, H. D. (Capt. late
Camerons)   1/ 2/41
Mackie, J.   28/ 5/41

Lieutenants

Hamilton, D.   1/ 2/41
Blair, T. (Capt. late R. Scots.) 1/ 2/41
Lumsden, W. V., D.S.O., M.C.,
(Lt.-Col. ret. pay)   1/ 2/41
Campbell, D. M.C., (Capt. late
Seaforths)   1/ 2/41
Macpherson, T.   1/ 2/41
Montgomery, G.   1/ 2/41
Balfour, J. D.   1/ 2/41
Bower, J. A. (Lt. late Assam
Valley Lt. Horse)   1/ 2/41
Hamilton, J. G. H. (Hon. Brig.
Gen. ret. pay)   1/ 2/41

Lieutenants - contd.

Mackie, C. G. S. (Capt.
late Lab. Corps.)   1/ 2/41
Joss, M.B.   1/ 2/41
Carruth, J. K. (Flt./Cmdr.
late R.A.F.)   1/ 2/41
Shepherd, A.   1/ 2/41
Nicoll, J.S.   1/ 2/ 41
Scott-Duff, A. A., C.I.E.,
M.V.O. (Bt. Lt.-Col. late
Gordons)   1/ 2/41
Mackintosh, J. G.   1/ 2/41
Inkster, A. R.   1/ 2/41
Riddler, J. C., M.C. (Capt.
late Gordons)   1/ 2/41

2nd Lieutenants

Cochrane, J. H. (Capt. late
R. Scots)   1/ 2/41
Duguid-McCombie, W. M. D.S.O.,
(Col. late The Greys)   1/ 2/41
Brent, H. A. W.   1/ 2/41
Alexander, C. G. (Lt.-Col.
late Ind. Army)   1/ 2/41
Mitchell, J.   1/ 2/41
Anderson, A. (2/Lt. late R.A.F.) 1/ 2/41
Will, R. W.   1/ 2/41
Pirie, J. T. (Lt. late Gordons) 1/ 2/41
Robertson, R. M.   1/ 2/41
Ross, R. B.   1/ 2/41
Forbes, J. A.   1/ 2/41
Cooper, T. L.   1/ 2/41
Charles, G. E.   1/ 2/41
Robertson, J. (2/Lt. late T.A.) 1/ 2/41
Arbuthnott, The Visct. (2/Lt.
late W.G'ds.)   1/ 2/41
Smart, W. F.   1/ 2/41
Dyker, A.   1/ 2/41
Sangster, A.   1/ 2/41
Bissett, P. (Lt. late Gordons) 1/ 2/41
Briggs, A. J. M.   1/ 2/41
Parsons, E. G. S.   15/ 6/41
Purvis, L. S.   21/ 6/41

Adjutant & Quarter-Master

Medical Officer

Sinclair, Maj. R. M.B.,
(Capt. late R.A.M.C.)   1/ 2/41

4th CITY OF ABERDEEN BATTALION

Lt.-Colonel
Anderson, A. S. M.B.E., (Capt.
late Gordons)   1/ 2/41

Majors
Sutherland, J. M.B.E., (Maj.
late Gordons)   1/ 2/41
Fiddess, J. (Capt. late
Ind. Army)   1/ 2/41
Smith, M. M.C., (Capt. late T.A.) 1/ 2/41
Macdiarmid, J. D. (Maj. late T.A.) 1/ 2/41
Milne, C. N. C. V.D., (Maj.
late Can. Mil. Forces)   1/ 2/41
Gray, M. H. (Capt. late R.L.I.) 1/ 2/41
Rhind, W. M.C., (Capt. late T.A.) 1/ 2/41

Captains
Bishop, T. R.   1/ 2/41
Reid, W. S., M.M.   1/ 2/41
Forbes, C. D. (2/Lt. late
Gen. List T.A.)   1/ 2/41
Ramsay, C. (2/Lt. late R.
Berks. R.)   1/ 2/41
Ingram, A. L. (Lt. late Bedfs &
Herts R.)   1/ 2/41
Adam, T. L. (Capt. late Gordons.) 1/ 2/41
Rollo, R. L. (Lt. late R.E.)   1/ 2/41
Doeg, J. (Lt. late T.A.)   1/ 2/41
Aitken, R. S. (Lt. late R.F.A.) 1/ 2/41

Lieutenants
Macintyre, A. (Capt. late
A. & S.H.)   1/ 2/41
Cheyne, W. T.   1/ 2/41
Nicol, A.   1/ 2/41
Fleetham, J. O.   1/ 2/41
Roe, F. C.   1/ 2/41
Sutherland, J. J. (Lt. late
Gordons)   1/ 2/41
Law, D. D. (Lt. late Gordons)   1/ 2/41
Westland, G. W., (Capt. late
Gordons)   1/ 2/41
Ross, J. L. J. (2/Lt. late
R.A.F.)   1/ 2/41
Webster, J. (Lt. late R.E.)   1/ 2/41
Stewart, R. R.   1/ 2/41

Lieutenants - contd.
Fearby, S. A. (Capt. late
S.Wales Bord.)   1/ 2/41
Mackie, D. G.   1/ 2/41
Stroud, G. D. W.   1/ 2/41
Adam, H. A. W.   1/ 2/41
McIvor, J. M.C., M.M.,
(Capt. late Can. Mil. Forces)   1/ 2/41
Paterson, A. A. A. D.S.O.,
M.C., (Maj. late R.A.)   1/ 2/41
Cormack, A. C.   30/ 7/41
Campbell, J. D.   31/ 7/41

2nd Lieutenants
Jones, D. J.   1/ 2/41
Miller, J. A.   1/ 2/41
Dunn, J. W. (2/Lt. late R.A.)   1/ 2/41
Blyth, H. J.   1/ 2/41
Reid, J. (late R.N.)   1/ 2/41
Hunter, S. J. (Lt. late R.E.)   1/ 2/41
King, J. C.   1/ 2/41
Bruce, A. (Lt. late R.A.S.C.)   1/ 2/41
Skinner, G. C.   1/ 2/41
Logie, D.   1/ 2/41
Main, P. T.   1/ 2/41
Jackson, W. M. (2/Lt. late T.A.) 11/ 1/41
Alexander, J.   1/ 2/41
Macdonald, A. R. (Lt. late
R.F.A.)   1/ 2/41
Bain, R.   1/ 2/41
Williams, I., D.C.M.   1/ 2/41
Archibald, C. B.   1/ 2/41
Gordon, J. (2/Lt. late
Lincoln R.)   1/ 2/41
Robinson, S. H.   1/ 2/41
Forsyth, J. M.   1/ 2/41
Milne, A.   1/ 2/41
Sellar, J. G.   1/ 2/41

Adjutant & Quarter-Master
Reid, Capt. (actg. 27/2/41)
W.P., Gen. List. Inf.   27/ 2/41

Medical Officer
Duncan, Maj. G. L. M.B., (Lt.-
Col. late Ind. Med. Serv.)   1/ 2/41

5th ABERDEENSHIRE BATTALION

Lt.-Colonel
Duff, G. B., D.S.O. (Lt.-Col.
ret. pay)   1/ 2/41

Lieutenants - contd.
McIntosh, J. S.	1/ 2/41
Leggat, A. B.	1/ 2/41
McDonald, Sir James G., K.B.E.	1/ 2/41
Arbuthnot-Leslie, W. (Lt. late	
S. G'ds.)	1/ 2/41
Low, R.	1/ 2/41
Giles, W.	1/ 2/41
Lessells, J.	1/ 2/41

Majors
Macaulay, A. M.C., (Capt. late Camerons)	1/ 2/41
Loutit, J. H., M.C. (Capt. late A. & S.H.)	1/ 2/41
Leggat, W. K., M.C. (Capt. late Gordons)	1/ 2/41
Manson, A. (Capt. late Gordons)	1/ 2/41

2nd Lieutenant
Whyte, A. B. (Capt. late
Gordons)   1/ 2/41

Captains
Murray, P. M., O.B.E., M.C.,
(Maj. late Seaforths)   1/ 2/41

Adjutant & Quarter-Master
Spence, Capt. G. T. Gordons,
T.A.   23/ 5/41

Lieutenants
Hutcheon, W. M. (2/Lt. late R.A.S.C.)	1/ 2/41
Eaton, J. D.	1/ 2/41
Cruikshank, A. A.	1/ 2/41
Cowieson, J. T.	1/ 2/41
Fyfe, C. F.	1/ 2/41
Taylor, R.	1/ 2/41
Calder, J. B. (Lt. late R.A.M.C.)	1/ 2/41

Medical Officer
Hunter, Maj. J., M.B.   1/ 2/41

NORTH HIGHLAND AREA - contd.

NO.3 ZONE (ABERDEEN) - contd.

6th ABERDEENSHIRE BATTALION
(12th G.P.O.)

Lt.-Colonel

Humphreys, W. P.	1/ 2/41

Majors

Perryman, C. F.	1/ 2/41
Reid, J. A.	1/ 2/41
Ramsay, M. W.	1/ 2/41
Mackay, K. C. M.	1/ 2/41

Captains

Macdonald, A. (Lt. late T.A.)	1/ 2/41
Cameron, J. J. W. E. K., M.C. (Capt. late R. Fus.)	1/ 2/41
Macdonald, J.	1/ 2/41
Bremner, R. C.	1/ 2/41
Hodge, J. D. M.	1/ 2/41
Wood, F.	1/ 2/41

Lieutenants

Davidson, J. P.	1/ 2/41
Barnes, A. F.	1/ 2/41
Morley, J. E.	1/ 2/41
Duncan, T. S.	1/ 2/41
Quin, J.	1/ 2/41
McLeod, M. G.	1/ 2/41
Livingston, J. G.	1/ 2/41

Lieutenants - contd.

Turner, A. G.	1/ 2/41
Hall, H.	1/ 2/41
Fraser, W.	1/ 2/41
Campbell, J. T. (Lt. late Seaforth)	1/ 2/41
McClelland, W. C., D.C.M.	1/ 2/41
Matheson, N.	1/ 2/41
McCallum, N. M.	1/ 2/41

2nd Lieutenants

Mckerlie, D. C.	1/ 2/41
Mckechnie, J.	1/ 2/41
Easton, A. L.	1/ 2/41

Adjutant & Quarter-Master

Medical Officer

NORTH HIGHLAND AREA - contd.

NO.3 ZONE (ABERDEEN) - contd.

7th CITY OF ABERDEEN (WORKS) BATTALION

Lt.-Colonel

Ledingham, R. M., T.D., (Maj. late T.A. Res.)	1/ 2/41

Majors

Cozens-Hardy, S. N. (Capt. late Norfolk R.)	1/ 2/41
Davidson, J. K.	1/ 2/41
Cross, T. E.	1/ 2/41
Hale, C. W.	1/ 2/41

Captains

Calvert, R. H.	1/ 2/41
Lewis, A. H. S. (Capt. late R.E.)	1/ 2/41
Scott, A. M.	1/ 2/41
Williamson, F.	1/ 2/41
Keith, A.	1/ 2/41
Robertson, D. G.	1/ 2/41
Campbell, A. J.	1/ 2/41

Lieutenants

Edwards, L. (2/Lt. late R.A.F.)	1/ 2/41
Davison, D. W.	1/ 2/41
Hill, H. B.	1/ 2/41
Norrie, W. (Lt. late R.A.F.)	1/ 2/41
Murray, J.	1/ 2/41
Greig, C. W. R.	1/ 2/41
Watt, A. R.	1/ 2/41
Dickson, A. M.	1/ 2/41
Grant, A. G.	1/ 2/41

2nd Lieutenants

Beaton, I. R.	1/ 2/41
Kirkland, H. G. (Lt. late R.A.F.)	1/ 2/41
Johnston, A. G.	1/ 2/41

Adjutant & Quarter-Master

Medical Officer

Semple, Maj. R., O.B.E. (Maj. late R.A.M.C.)	1/ 2/41

8th N. & S. HIGHLAND AREA (4th L.N.E.R.) BATTALION

Lt.-Colonel

Farr, L. (Lt. late R.A.)	1/ 2/41

Majors

Cruikshank, R.	1/ 2/41
Duff, J.	1/ 2/41
Dargie, J. L.	1/ 2/41

Adjutant & Quarter-Master

Medical Officer

56455-3(23)

SOUTH HIGHLAND AREA

General Staff Officer 1st grade   Renny - Tailyour, Col. J. W., D.S.O.,
     ret. pay (Res. of Off.)   9/ 7/40

NO. 1 ZONE (ANGUS & DUNDEE)

Commander   Maitland, Col. G. R., D.S.O.,
     (Lt.-Col. ret. pay)
     (Lt.-Col. late T.A.)   1/ 2/41

Assistant to Zone Commander   Guild, Maj. A. M., D.S.O., T.D.,
     (Lt.-Col. late Black Watch)   1/ 2/41

Territorial Army Association }   Dundee & Angus T.A. Association,
administering   8, South Lindsay Street, Dundee.

1st ANGUS BATTALION

Lt.-Colonel

Dalhousie, The Earl of (Maj. late T.A.)	1/ 2/41

Majors

Walker, C. W.	1/ 2/41
Macgregor, J. St. C., O.B.E., (Lt.-Col. late R.A.)	1/ 2/41
Wilson, D. M., (Lt. late Black Watch)	1/ 2/41
Adler, B. I. H., O.B.E., (Lt.-Col. late Indian Army)	1/ 2/41
Maclagan, J.	1/ 2/41
Ogilvie, D. D., (Maj. late T.A.)	1/ 2/41
Chapman, W. J., (Capt. late Cameronians)	1/ 2/41
Calder, W. G., D.C.M.	4/ 8/41

Captains

Hastings, A. S.	1/ 2/41
Duke, A. W., T.D. (Maj. T.A. Res.)	1/ 2/41
Smith, J.	1/ 2/41
Inglis, T. (Lt. late T.A.)	1/ 2/41
Shanks, F. (Capt. late Black Watch)	1/ 2/41

Lieutenants

Morgan, D., M.C., (Lt. late H.L.I.)	1/ 2/41
Milne, D. S.	1/ 2/41
Muncie, W. R.	1/ 2/41
Taylor, J.	1/ 2/41
Davidson, J. D.	1/ 2/41
Beattie, G.	1/ 2/41
Hogg, A. G.	1/ 2/41
Mangie, J.	1/ 2/41
Berwick, D. B.	1/ 2/41
Smart, G. B., (Lt. late Black Watch)	1/ 2/41
Reid, W. A., (Capt. late R.F.A.)	1/ 2/41
Robertson, A. K., M.C., (Capt. late R.F.C.)	1/ 2/41
Fyfe, J. M. D. Y.	1/ 2/41

Lieutenants - contd.

Kaye, G. L.	1/ 2/41
Stewart, J. W.	1/ 2/41
McLaughlan, W.	1/ 2/41
Urquhart, D. D., (Maj. late T.A.)	1/ 2/41
Baxter, D., M.C., (Lt. late Black Watch)	1/ 2/41
Fenton, P. L.	1/ 2/41
Ramsay, R. O.	1/ 2/41
Cochrane, J.	1/ 2/41
Hume, R. M., (Lt. late Black Watch)	1/ 2/41
Robertson, W. H.	1/ 2/41
Turner, G.	1/ 2/41
Ferrier, H. A., (Lt. late Black Watch)	1/ 2/41
Edwards, S.	1/ 2/41
Allison, R., (2/Lt. late R.A.F.)	4/ 7/41
Stevens, D. W.	15/ 7/41

2nd Lieutenants

Lindsay, J., (Lt. late T.A.)	1/ 2/41
Smart, G. G. J.	1/ 2/41
Henderson, J. F.	1/ 2/41
Nairn, A. F.	1/ 2/41
Bryce. J.	1/ 2/41
Davidson, J.	1/ 2/41
McEwan, W.	1/ 2/41
McConnell, T. E.	1/ 2/41
Ferguson, W. H.	1/ 2/41
Edwards, G.	1/ 2/41
Duncan, E. B., (Capt. late R.T.R.)	1/ 2/41
Ashford, R.	1/ 2/41
Norrie, D. S.	1/ 2/41
Mitchell, W. G.	1/ 2/41
Monro, A. J. F., O.B.E. (Capt. late Gordons)	1/ 2/41
Johnston, W. D.	1/ 2/41
Rushton, H. L.	15/ 7/41

Adjutant & Quarter-Master

Medical Officer

Lindeberg, Maj., E. W., M.B., (Lt. late R.A.F.)	1/ 2/41

2nd ANGUS BATTALION

Lt.-Colonel
Baxter, G. L. D.S.O., (Lt.-Col.
ret. pay)   1/ 2/41

Majors
Neish, C. F. I. (Lt. late
Black Watch)   1/ 2/41
Smith, J. A., M.C. (Capt. late
Black Watch)   1/ 2/41
Munro, Sir Thomas T. A.
Bt., (2/Lt. late G. Gds.)   1/ 2/41
Methuen, C. M. (2/Lt. late
Black Watch)   1/ 2/41
Melville, J. H. (Lt. late
H.L.I.)   1/ 2/41

Captains
Kilgour, D. (Lt. late R.S. Fus.) 1/ 2/41
Ogilvy, R. D. B.   1/ 2/41
Easson, G. L. (Capt. late Rifle
Bde.)   1/ 2/41
Milne, T. M.C., (Capt. late
K.A. Rif.)   1/ 2/41
Maclean, J. C.   6/ 8/41
Hay, D. L. H.   6/ 8/41
Logan, R.   6/ 8/41
Waters, H. B., O.B.E.   6/ 8/41

Lieutenants
Johnstone-Brodie, C. H. C.,
T.D. (Capt. late R.F.A.)   1/ 2/41
Callander, D.   1/ 2/41
Marshall, W. L.   1/ 2/41
Watson, J. M.   1/ 2/41
Archie, A. R.   1/ 2/41
Whitton, A. M.   1/ 2/41

56455-3(25)

Lieutenants - contd.
Anderson, G. C.   1/ 2/41
Fraser, J.   1/ 2/41
Fraser, J. P. M.C. (2/Lt.
late K.O.Y.L.I.)   1/ 2/41
Wilson, W. S.   1/ 2/41
Adamson, M. W.   1/ 2/41
Mackenzie, W. A. (Lt-Col.
late Transvaal Scottish)   1/ 2/41
Mackenzie, W. S. (Lt. late
Gordons)   1/ 2/41
Murray, J. (Lt. late R.F.A.)   1/ 2/41
Moyes, D. S. (Capt. Late T.A.)   1/ 2/41
Pattullo, D. J.   1/ 2/41

2nd Lieutenants
Tosh, A.   1/ 2/41
Hay, A.   1/ 2/41
Duncan, J.   1/ 2/41
Rorison, H. G. G.   1/ 2/41
Maxwell, G.   1/ 2/41
Liddell, D.   1/ 2/41
Mudie, M.   1/ 2/41
Ogilvy, W. (Lt. late R.G.A.)   1/ 2/41

Adjutant & Quarter-Master

Medical Officer
Myles, Maj. D., (Lt. late
R. Signals)   1/ 2/41

33

1st CITY OF DUNDEE BATTALION

Lt.-Colonel
Sillars, D. (Maj. ret. T.A.)   1 / 2/41

Majors
Rettie, A. (Lt. late R.N.V.R.)   1 / 2/41
Horswell, C. H. (Capt. late
Gordons.)   1 / 2/41
Forsyth, J. C., M.C. (Lt. late
R.A.F.)   1 / 2/41
Fraser, A. (Capt. late R.A.S.C.)   1 / 2/41
Yates, C. T.   1 / 2/41

Captains
Sutherland, C. A. (Lt. late
Black Watch)   1 / 2/41
Watson, J. Y. (Lt. late
R.F.C.)   1 / 2/41
Pryde, R. (Lt. late Loyal R.)   1 / 2/41
Brown, J. S.   1 / 2/41
Ruthven, A. B., (Capt. late
A. & S.H.)   1 / 2/41
Robb, J. M., (Lt. late Gordons)   1 / 2/41

Lieutenants
Hunter, R. (Lt. late R.F.A.)   1 / 2/41
Smith, R. A. (Lt. late Gordons)   1 / 2/41
Carlton, H. J. (Lt. late T.A.)   1 / 2/41
Hood, J. T.   1 / 2/41
Steven, W.   1 / 2/41
Black, A. M.   1 / 2/41
Deas, E. H., M.C. (Capt. late
T.A.)   1 / 2/41
Pratt, A. S.   1 / 2/41
Hunt, R. G.   1 / 2/41
Thomson, S. C., M.C. (Maj.
late M.G. Corps.)   1 / 2/41
McKay, A. D. D.   1 / 2/41
Taylor, R. A. (2/Lt. late
King's Own R.)   1 / 2/41
Valentine, R. L. H. (2/Lt.
late R.A.F.)   1 / 2/41

Lieutenants - contd.
Cree, T. M.   1 / 2/41
Sturrock, H.   1 / 2/41
Brown, D. H.   1 / 2/41
McLaren, T.   1 / 2/41
Dorward, T. P.   23/6/41

2nd Lieutenants
Kidd, W. D. (Lt. late R.G.A.)   1 / 2/41
Fyffe, D. R. (Capt. late R.T.R.)   1 / 2/41
Butterfield, J. E.   1 / 2/41
Anderson, J. S. (Lt. late
M.G. Corps)   1 / 2/41
McFarlane, J.   1 / 2/41
Brown, C. E.   1 / 2/42
Ferguson, G.   1 / 2/41
Mitchell, W. W. (Lt. late
Black Watch)   1 / 2/41
Cleghorn, C. R. M.C., (Capt.
late Midd'x. R.)   1 / 2/41
Reid, W. G. (Lt. late R.A.S.C.)   1 / 2/41
Gray, N., A.F.C., D.C.M., M.M.
(Lt. late R.N.A.S.)   1 / 2/41
Murdoch, G. A.   1 / 2/41
Milne, W.   1 / 2/41
Falconer, C., M.M.   1 / 2/41
Gordon, A. (Lt. late Gordons)   23/ 6/41

Adjutant & Quarter-Master

Medical Officer

SOUTH HIGHLAND AREA — contd.

NO. 1 ZONE (ANGUS & DUNDEE) — contd.

2nd CITY OF DUNDEE BATTALION	
Lt—Colonel	
Smith, S. R. (Lt. late R.A.)	1/ 2/41
Majors	
Thyne, J. G. F.	1/ 2/41
Parker, G. C.	1/ 2/41
Duncan, J. B.	1/ 2/41
McIntosh, H. W., M.C. (Late R. Ir. Rif.)	1/ 2/41
Leuchars, J. W. (Capt. late Black Watch)	1/ 2/41
Captains	
McKirdy, W.	1/ 2/41
Wooler, J.	1/ 2/41
Keith, L. S.	1/ 2/41
Soutar, P. A. (Capt. late R. Scots.)	1/ 2/41
Lieutenants	
Weddell, J. H.	1/ 2/41
McQueen, H.	1/ 2/41
Maxwell, D.	1/ 2/41
Mudie, G. G.	1/ 2/41
Preston, J.	1/ 2/41
Campbell, J. D.	1/ 2/41
Moffat, J.	1/ 2/41
Casey, T. A'B.	1/ 2/41
Scott, A. D.	1/ 2/41
McIntosh, J.	1/ 2/41
Lochrie, C. M.	1/ 2/41
Thompson, A. E.	1/ 6/41
2nd Lieutenants	
Morrison, A.	1/ 2/41
Stevenson, O. S.	1/ 2/41
Whitton, A.	1/ 2/41
Vine, R. H.	1/ 2/41
McDougall, J., D.C.M., M.M.	1/ 2/41
Clark, C. S.	1/ 2/41
Cruickshank, A. G.	1/ 2/41
Gill, F. M.	1/ 2/41
Adjutant & Quarter—Master	
Mitchell, Capt. (actg. 30/5/41) G.A.,Gen. List Inf.	30/ 5/41
Medical Officer	
Thomson, Maj., J., M.B., F.R.C.P.	1/ 2/41

56455-3(27)

3rd CITY OF DUNDEE BATTALION (13th G.P.O.)	
Lt.-Colonel	
Rae, R. B. (2/Lt. late R.E.)	1/ 2/41
Majors	
Oram, W. W.	1/ 2/41
Heyde, D., O.B.E., (Maj. late R.E.)	1/ 2/41
Smith, S. J.	1/ 2/41
Walmsley, J.	1/ 2/41
Captains	
McIntyre, A. (Lt. late A. & S.H.)	1/ 2/41
Donaldson, J., M.M.	1/ 2/41
Laurence, H. L. H.	1/ 2/41
Lieutenants	
Mackie, S., (Lt. late K.O.S.B.)	1/ 2/41
McLaren, W.	1/ 2/41
Mathewson, J. M.	1/ 2/41
Mason, D. W.	1/ 2/41
Ferguson, D.	1/ 2/41
McCormick, R. M.	1/ 2/41
Thomson, H.H., M.C., (Capt. late H.L.I.)	1/ 2/41
Whiston, J. W.	1/ 2/41
Cameron, J. W., D.C.M.	1/ 2/41

2nd Lieutenants

Adjutant & Quarter—Master

Medical Officer

Commander	Hunter, Col. P. C., **T.D.**, (**Bt. Col.** ret. **T.A.**)	1/ 2/41
Staff Officer	Innes, Capt. S. A., **D.S.O.** (**Lt.** **Col. late Black Watch**)	1/ 2/41
Chief Guide	Richmond, Capt., **C.M.**. (**Maj.** **late Black Watch**)	1/ 2/41
Intelligence Officer	Hamilton-Smith, Capt. R. H. (**Lt.-Col. Black Watch**)	5/ 8/41
Territorial Army Association } administering	County of Perth T.A. Association, 3, Kinnoul Street, Perth.	

1st PERTHSHIRE BATTALION

Lt.-Colonel

Butter, C. A. J., **O.B.E.**, (**Col. late R.A.F.**)	1/ 2/41

Majors

Drew, J. S., **C.B.**, **D.S.O.**, **M.C.**, (**Maj.-Gen. ret. pay**)	1/ 2/41
Macnaughton, B. A., (**Capt. late A. & S.H.**)	1/ 2/41
Paterson, W. E.	1/ 2/41

Captains

Lieutenants

Georgeson, E. H. M., **M.C.**, (**Capt. late R. Scots.**)	1/ 2/41
Matthewson, B. A., (**Capt. late Camerons**)	1/ 2/41
Davidson, J. S.	1/ 2/41
Morrison, J. R.	1/ 2/41
Brander, J. S. H.	1/ 2/41
Fleming, R. S. T., (**Flt./Lt. late R.A.F.**)	1/ 2/41
Fergusson, E. J., (**Lt.-Cmdr. R.N.**)	1/ 2/41

Lieutenants - contd.

Esler, D. G.	1/ 2/41
Boyce, J.	1/ 2/41
Stewart, F. J.	1/ 2/41
Macleod, A.	1/ 8/41
Mellor, J. E.	1/ 8/41

2nd Lieutenants

Macarthur, J.	1/ 2/41
Fraser, J. C.	1/ 2/41
Macdowell, G. A. D., (**Capt. late R.F.A.**)	1/ 2/41
Mackenzie, H. A.	1/ 2/41
Hughes, D. W.	1/ 2/41
Finlayson, W.	1/ 2/41

Adjutant & Quarter-Master

Medical Officer

SOUTH HIGHLAND AREA - contd.

No. 2 ZONE (PERTHSHIRE) - contd.

2nd PERTHSHIRE BATTALION	
Lt.-Colonel	
Nunn, T. H. C., D.S.O., (Lt.-Col. ret. pay)	1/ 2/41
Majors	
Balfour, F. K., (Lt. late Black Watch)	1/ 2/41
Robinson, E. H., (2/Lt. late T.A.)	1/ 2/41
Captains	
McDonald, W. S., (2/Lt. late R.A.F.)	1/ 2/41
Lieutenants	
Conacher, C. M.	1/ 2/41
Bell, N. T.	1/ 2/41
Denholm, J. D.	1/ 2/41
Menzies, W. N. G. (2/Lt. late Black Watch)	1/ 2/41
Taylor, D., (Lt. late Camerons)	1/ 2/41
Young, D. E.	1/ 2/41
Glass, W. M.	1/ 2/41
Bruges, W. I.	1/ 2/41
Pattullo, I. N.	1/ 2/41
Macdonald, G. F., (Capt. late H.L.I.)	1/ 2/41
Greenhill, W.	1/ 2/41
Addie, J. A.	1/ 2/41
McGill, D. (2/Lt. late R. Scots.)	1/ 2/41
Anderson, J. M. (2/Lt. late R.T.R.)	1/ 2/41
Calder, G. G., T.D., (Capt. late Lovat Scouts)	1/ 2/41
Scott, J.	1/ 2/41
Macgregor, J.	1/ 2/41
Herd, J.	1/ 2/41
Thom, G. B.	1/ 2/41
Thomas, B. B. (Lt. late A.I.F.)	1/ 2/41
Tatton, E., (2/Lt. late Welch R.)	1/ 2/41
Clark, W.	1/ 2/41
2nd Lieutenants	
Taylor, J.	1/ 2/41
Fordyce, W. R.	1/ 2/41
Nicoll, W. S. (Lt. late M.G. Corps)	1/ 2/41
Lowson, J. T.	1/ 2/41

Adjutant & Quarter-Master

Medical Officer

3rd PERTHSHIRE BATTALION	
Lt.-Colonel	
Bell, F. A., M.C., (Capt. late T.A.)	1/ 2/41
Majors	
McIntyre, J. C., M.C. (Capt. late Black Watch)	1/ 2/41
Main, A. D. C. (2/Lt. late T.A.)	1/ 2/41
Mansfield, The Earl of (Lt. late Black Watch)	1/ 2/41
Roberts, Sir James D., Bt.	1/ 2/41
Low, J.	1/ 6/41
Captains	
Holland, J. E. D., D.S.O., M.C. (Lt.-Col. late 5th D.G.)	1/ 2/41
Daldy, F. G., (T.A. Gen. List)	1/ 2/41
Reid, A., (Lt. late R.E.)	1/ 2/41
Sellar, R. J. B. (Capt. late H.L.I.)	1/ 2/41
Lieutenants	
McLaren, M., M.C. (Lt. late Black Watch)	1/ 2/41
Scott, G., M.C., (Lt. late Black Watch)	1/ 2/41
Rossiter, J. R.	1/ 2/41
Anderson, G. F.	1/ 2/41
Brown, A. O.	1/ 2/41
Taylor, J. L. M.	1/ 2/41
Hammond, W. P.	1/ 2/41
Powrie, W.	1/ 2/41
Henderson, W.	1/ 2/41
Frew, J. G. R.	1/ 2/41
Gangster, W. H.	1/ 2/41
McOwan, G. (Lt. late R.S.Fus.)	1/ 2/41
Liddell, J.	1/ 2/41
Beveridge, J. D. (Capt. late N. Stafford R.)	1/ 2/41
Fraser, W. L.	1/ 2/41
Thomson, G. D.	25/ 7/41
2nd Lieutenants	
Slessor, W. F.	1/ 2/41
Mills, R. C.	1/ 2/41
Millar, C. M. H.	12/ 6/41
Falconer, J. M. (2/Lt. late R.A.F.)	18/ 6/41

Adjutant & Quarter-Master

Medical Officer

43-44

4th PERTHSHIRE BATTALION

Lt.-Colonel

Mackenzie, J. M. D.	1/ 2/41

Majors

Bell, A., (Capt. late Worcs. R.)	1/ 2/41
Niven, A. C.	1/ 2/41
Burrell, T. M. (Maj. late T.A.)	1/ 2/41
Howie, A. (Lt. late R. Scots.)	1/ 2/41
Wright, A. A. K.	1/ 2/41
Rae, D. J.	28/ 7/41

Captains

Todd, J. C. (Lt. late R.A.F.)	1/ 2/41
Macpherson, C. F. (Maj. late T.A.)	1/ 2/41
Cox, E. H. M. (Lt. late R. Mar.)	1/ 2/41
Miller, W. S.	1/ 2/41

Lieutenants

Pilcher, W. H., (Capt. late Black Watch)	1/ 2/41
Thomas, G. F., M.M.	1/ 2/41
Martin, J. T., (Lt. late T.A.)	1/ 2/41
Lamond, A. D. (Lt. late R.A.S.C.)	1/ 2/41
Williamson, R.	1/ 2/41
Garrett, C.	1/ 2/41
Stewart, P. C.	1/ 2/41
MacBeath, A.	1/ 2/41
Piper, W. G.	1/ 2/41
Mackie, A. E.	8/ 4/41
Maclean, A. J.	8/ 6/41
Stiver, C. W.	8/ 8/41

2nd Lieutenants

Scott, M. (Lt. late T.A.)	1/ 2/41
Sheriffs, J. F. S. (2/Lt. late R.A.)	1/ 2/41
Meikle, T. J. (Lt. late T.A.)	1/ 2/41
Macnicol, W.	1/ 2/41
Melville, K.	1/ 2/41
Pattullo, G. B.	1/ 2/41
Murray, W.	1/ 2/41
Hope, D. S.	24/ 6/41
Moody, R. H.	24/ 6/41
Sutton, F. W.	24/ 7/41

Adjutant & Quarter-Master

Medical Officer

5th PERTHSHIRE BATTALION

Lt.-Colonel

Stirling, P. D., O.B.E., M.C., (Maj. late T.A.)	1/ 2/41

Majors

Spooner, C. C., D.S.O., (Lt.-Col. late Essex R.)	1/ 2/41
McGrigor, A. M. (Capt. late T.A.)	1/ 2/41
Campbell-Colquhoun, A. J. (Capt. late Camerons)	1/ 2/41
Wilson, Sir James R., Bt. (Capt. late T.A.)	1/ 2/41
Macgregor-Whitton, A. E. H., (Maj. late R.S.Fus.)	1/ 2/41
Wallace, J. E. F., (Capt. late M.G. Corps)	1/ 2/41
Donald, A., (Maj. late Ind. Army)	1/ 2/41

Captains

Darling, J. A. (Maj. late T.A.)	1/ 2/41
Moffat, G. K. (Maj. late T.A.)	1/ 2/41
Stradling, A. R. (Capt. late R.A.S.C.)	1/ 2/41
Bowser, D. C., O.B.E., (Capt. late R.A.S.C.)	1/ 2/41
Bain, R. D. (Maj. late R.A.O.C.)	1/ 2/41

Lieutenants

McCall, R. L., D.S.O., M.C. (Col. ret. pay) (Res. of Off.)	1/ 2/41
Pullar, J. L., O.B.E. (Maj. T.A. Res.)	1/ 2/41
Masterton, W. A.	1/ 2/41
Budd, H. H.	1/ 2/41
Titterington, T.	1/ 2/41
James, J. E.	1/ 2/41
Farquharson, H. H.	1/ 2/41
Kinnes, W. (Capt. late R.F.A.)	1/ 2/41
Hughes, T. H. (Capt. late R.E.)	1/ 2/41
Currie, J. (Capt. late A. Cyclist Corps.)	1/ 2/41
Findlay, J. B.	1/ 2/41
Cross, A.	1/ 2/41
McQueen, J.	1/ 2/41
Chisholm, H. W.	1/ 2/41
Ballingall, S. (Capt. late R.A.S.C.)	1/ 2/41

2nd Lieutenants

Ward, D. W.	1/ 2/41
Macgregor of Macgregor, Sir Malcolm, Bt., C.B., C.M.G., (Capt. ret. R.N.)	1/ 2/41
Spence, F., (Lt. late R.N.V.R.)	1/ 2/41
Ferguson, F. O.B.E.	1/ 2/41
Mackay, J. W.	1/ 2/41
Grahame, M. J. H.	1/ 2/41
Dykes, J.	1/ 2/41
Muir, J.	1/ 2/41
Forrester, J.	1/ 2/41
McNaughton, A.	1/ 2/41

Adjutant & Quarter-Master

Medical Officer

SOUTH HIGHLAND AREA - contd.

No. 2 ZONE (PERTHSHIRE) - contd.

6th PERTHSHIRE BATTALION

Lt.-Colonel

Hunter, A. D., M.C., (Maj. late
R.A. Spec. Res.)   1/ 2/41

Majors

Gillies, W. L.   (Lt. late
Black Watch)   1/ 2/41
Young, G. C.   (Lt. late
R.T.R.)   1/ 2/41
Galbraith, J.   1/ 2/41

Captains

Hogg, C.   1/ 2/41
Grassie, J. T., D.S.O.,
M.B.E. (Capt. late Black
Watch)   1/ 2/41
Simpson, A. M. (Lt. Res.
of Off.)   1/ 2/41

Lieutenants

Gordon, R. J. M. (Lt. late
Gordons.)   .   1/ 2/41
Jackson, P. M. (2/Lt. late
Border R.)   1/ 2/41
Hugelshofer, J. B. .(Capt.
late K.O.S.B.)   1/ 2/41
McIntosh, A. P., M.M.
(2/Lt. late R.E.)   1/ 2/41
Marshall, J. V., M.C. (Capt.
late R.F.A.)   1/ 2/41
Renton, J. T.   1/ 2/41
Simms, J. C. W.   1/ 2/41
McLagan, W. D.   1/ 2/41
Ross, R.   1/ 2/41
Duncan, T.   1/ 2/41
McKerrell, L. M., D.C.M., M.M.   10/ 6/41
Meldrum, J.   13/ 6/41

Lieutenants - contd.

Angus, J. (2/Lt. late Ind.
Army)   24/ 8/41

2nd Lieutenants

Fraser, J. L.   1/ 2/41
Anderson, J., (2/Lt. late
R.A.F.)   10/ 6/41
Brough, P. S., M.M.   10/ 6/41
Grahame, G., (2/Lt. late
M.G.Corps.)   10/ 6/41
McCowan, D. M.   10/ 6/41
Jeffrey, G. M., (Lt. late
H.L.I.)   10/ 6/41
Raitt, D.   10/ 6/41
Govan, W. F.   10/ 6/41
Aitken, W. T. B.   10/ 6/41
Mayo, J.   10/ 6/41

Adjutant & Quarter-Master
Cooper, Capt. (actg. 24/2/41)
K. E., Gen. List Inf.   24/ 2/41

Medical Officer

SOUTH HIGHLAND AREA – contd.

NO. 3 ZONE (FIFE & KINROSS-SHIRE)

Commander	Elgin & Kincardine, Col. The Earl of, K.T., C.M.G., T.D. 16/ 6/41
Second in Command	Chalmer, Lt.-Col. F. G., D.S.O., M.C. (Col. ret. pay) (Res. of Off.) 1/ 2/41
	McPherson, Maj. J., D.S.O.,
Assistants to Zone Commander	T.D., (Bt.-Col. late R.A.) 1/ 2/41
	Christie, Capt., R. L.,
	(Lt. late York R.) 1/ 2/41
Signal Officer	Brownlee, Capt., W. D.
	(Capt. late R.A.F.) 1/ 2/41
Chief Guide Officer	Timms, Capt. G. 1/ 2/41
Liaison Officer	Lindsay, Lt. W. L. 1/ 2/41
Weapon Training Officer	Dymcock, Lt. L. B. 1/ 2/11
Pigeon Officer	Beavers, Lt. T. 1/ 2/41
Territorial Army Association administering	County of Fife T.A. Association, Hunter Street, Kirkcaldy.

1st FIFE BATTALION

Lt.-Colonel

Mackie, D. G.	(Lt. late T.A.)	1/ 2/41

Majors

Calder, A. J.	1/ 2/41
Gold, W. R.	1/ 2/41
Ferguson, D. (Lt. late M.G. Corps)	1/ 2/41
Laing, J.	1/ 2/41

Captains

Liddle, G.	1/ 2/41
Swinton, J.	1/ 2/41
Gray, W.	1/ 2/41
Todd, J., (Lt. late R. Scots)	1/ 2/41
Syme, J. T.	1/ 2/41
Gibb, A. M.	1/ 2/41

Lieutenants

Roger, C. A.	1/ 2/41
Melville, J. (Lt. late R.G.A.)	1/ 2/41
Dunning, R. C. (Lt. late Seaforth)	1/ 2/41
Adamson, W. B.	1/ 2/41
Piper, J. N.	1/ 2/41
Gibb, J.	1/ 2/41
Hoggan, A. G.	1/ 2/41
Bisset McIntosh R.	1/ 2/41
McLaren, J.	1/ 2/41
Buttercase, D. L.	1/ 2/41
Adamson, A.	1/ 2/41
Allan, J. (2/Lt. R. Scots)	1/ 2/41

Lieutenants – contd.

Bright, G. F.	1/ 2/41
Wilson, T. F.	1/ 2/41
Chalmers, W. B.	1/ 2/41
Skene, P. G. M., O.B.E. (Lt.-Col. late Black Watch)	1/ 2/41
Graham, J.	1/ 2/41
McDonald, J., M.M.	1/ 2/41
Buttercase, A.	1/ 2/41
McCraw, W.	4/ 6/41

2nd Lieutenants

Waddell, J., M.M.	1/ 2/41
Thomson, W. H.	1/ 2/41
Stewart, J.	1/ 2/41
Clark, J.	1/ 2/41
Dowie, G.	1/ 2/41
Stirrat, J.	1/ 2/41
Arbuckle, J.	1/ 2/41
Adams, T.	1/ 2/41
Lockhart, R.	1/ 2/41
Richie, J. A.	1/ 2/41
Harper, S.	1/ 2/41
Downie, W.	1/ 2/41
Williamson, A.	1/ 2/41
Stewart, J. L.	1/ 2/41

Adjutant & Quarter-Master

Medical Officer

SOUTH HIGHLAND AREA - contd.
No. 3 ZONE (FIFE & KINROSS-SHIRE) - contd.

2nd FIFE BATTALION

Lt.-Colonel

Waters-Taylor, B. H. (Col.
ret. pay)   1/ 2/41

Majors
Erskine, Sir Thomas W. H. J., Bt.,
  D.S.O. (Lt.-Col. late Camerons)   1/ 2/41
Lowson, A. S. (Capt. late W.I.R.)   1/ 2/41
Simpson, J. G. (Capt. late Black
  Watch)   1/ 2/41
Adam, G. P.   1/ 2/41
Macewen, G. L., M.C. (Capt. late
  R.A.)   1/ 2/41
Maxwell, A.   14/ 5/41
Captains
Henderson, A. E. K.   1/ 2/41
Beaton, W. S.   1/ 2/41
Tindal, L., (Capt. late Black
  Watch)   1/ 2/41
Turnbull, J. M.   1/ 2/41

Lieutenants
Gray, W.   1/ 2/41
Ross, F. C. (Lt. late A. & S.H.)   1/ 2/41
Hope, E. S., M.C. (Lt. late
  North'd. Fus.)   1/ 2/41
Currie, N. T., (2/Lt. late Lab.
  Corps)   1/ 2/41
Thomson, N.   1/ 2/41
Donaldson, J. R.   1/ 2/41
Pratt, D.   1/ 2/41
Wilson, D. F.   1/ 2/41
Provan, A. J. C. (2/Lt. late T.A.)   1/ 2/41
Rose, H. J.   1/ 2/41
Mitchell, R.   1/ 2/41
Macdonald, W. C.   1/ 2/41
MacNiven, J.   1/ 2/41
Croll, G.   1/ 2/41
Niven, E. J. N.   1/ 2/41
Clark, J.   1/ 2/41
Snow, D. E.   1/ 2/41
Honeyman, A. M.   29/ 7/41

2nd Lieutenants
Inglis, A.   1/ 2/41
Sturrock, J. T.   1/ 2/41
Lang, J.   1/ 2/41
Gardiner, J.   1/ 2/41
Duff, D. W.   1/ 2/41
Graham, T.   1/ 2/41
Roger, F. W.   1/ 2/41

Adjutant & Quarter-Master

Medical Officer
Howden, Maj. T.   1/ 2/41

56455-3 (33)

3rd FIFE BATTALION

Lt.-Colonel
Nock, J. H., (2/Lt. late
  Serv. Bn. Rifle Bde.)   1/ 2/41

Majors
Edie, H. H.   1/ 2/41
Kelso, J. N.   1/ 2/41
Armour, M. D. S.   1/ 2/41
Inglis, J.   1/ 2/41
Cumming, A. F. (Lt. late R.E.)   1/ 2/41
Stewart, J. C.   15/ 5/41

Captains
Elder, A. M.   1/ 2/41
Whitelaw, R. S.   1/ 2/41
Burns, A. S.   1/ 2/41
Donaldson, G. V. (Lt. late
  Black Watch)   1/ 2/41
Thomson, H.   14/ 5/41
Lieutenants
Brown, J. A.   1/ 2/41
Hadow, Sir Raymond P., Knt.,
  C.I.E.   1/ 2/41
Inglis, J. A.   1/ 2/41
Blackery, D.   1/ 2/41
Miller, J.   1/ 2/41
Annandale, J. R.   1/ 2/41
Oswald, J.   1/ 2/41
Tunstall, R.   1/ 2/41
Carstairs, A.   1/ 2/41
Miller, A. S.   1/ 2/41
Bissett, T. B.   1/ 2/41
Rennie, J. R.   1/ 2/41
Foster, K. W. B., M.M.   1/ 2/41
Telford, R. K.   1/ 2/41
Tucker, R. F. (2/Lt. late
  Dorset R.)   1/ 2/41
Simmonds, R. C.   1/ 2/41
Hogg, W.   1/ 7/41

Adjutant & Quarter-Master

Medical Officer
Page, Maj. D. C. M., M.C.,
  (Maj. late R.A.M.C.)   1/ 2/41

SOUTH HIGHLAND AREA - contd.

No. 3 ZONE (FIFE & KINROSS-SHIRE) - contd.

4th FIFE BATTALION

Lt.-Colonel	
Mackenzie, A. A. (Capt. late T.A.)	1/ 2/41

Lieutenants - contd.	
Hall, D. M.	1/ 2/41
Simonson, J. C.	1/ 2/41

Majors	
Webster, J. L. M.C., (Capt. late R.A.)	1/ 2/41
Kinnear, J. S. (Lt. late R. Scots)	1/ 2/41
Howieson, A. F.	1/ 2/41
Ballantine, R.	1/ 2/41

2nd Lieutenants	
McKinlay, J.	1/ 2/41
Fisken, J. H. W.	1/ 2/41
Henderson, A. M.	1/ 2/41
Finnie, A.	1/ 2/41
Ferguson, W.	1/ 2/41
Rae, J.	1/ 2/41
Ritchie, D.	1/ 2/41
Drummond, G.	1/ 2/41
Briggs, T. D.	1/ 2/41
Ogilvie, D.	1/ 2/41
Weir, P.	1/ 2/41
Paterson, D.	1/ 2/41
Cumming, W. C.	1/ 2/41
Beveridge, J.	19/ 7/41
McPhail, D. (Capt. late Ind. Army)	21/ 7/41

Captains	
Drylie, W.	1/ 2/41
Porter, C.	1/ 2/41
Rankin, D.	1/ 2/41
Pitkeathly, J.	1/ 2/41
Tod, A. S., (Lt. late R. Fus.)	1/ 2/41
Bell, J. M.	1/ 2/41

Adjutant & Quarter-Master

Lieutenants	
Kidd, M. A.	1/ 2/41
Nicol, J. B.	1/ 2/41
Hood, A. W.	1/ 2/41
Russell, J.	1/ 2/41
Taylor, J.	1/ 2/41
Greig, T. D. (2/Lt. late Black Watch)	1/ 2/41
Ross, G. M.	1/ 2/41
Jinks, C.	1/ 2/41
Black, J. (2/Lt. late R.A.)	1/ 2/41
Farmer, A.	1/ 2/41

Medical Officer	
Johnstone, Maj., J. M. (Capt. late R.A.M.C.)	1/ 2/41

56455-3(34)

SOUTH HIGHLAND AREA - contd.

No. 3 ZONE (FIFE & KINROSS-SHIRE) - contd.

5th FIFE BATTALION

Lt.-Colonel
Macdonald, J. L. A., D.S.O.
(Lt.-Col. ret. pay)   1/ 2/41

Majors
Robertson, J.   1/ 2/41
Cunningham, J. G. (Capt.
late R.G.A.)   1/ 2/41
Tullis, G. S. (Capt. late
Black Watch)   1/ 2/41
Mackintosh, N. (2/Lt. late
R.T.R.)   1/ 2/41
Forrester, J. (2/Lt. late
M.G. Corps)   1/ 2/41
Whittam, A.   1/ 2/41

Captains
Meader, C. W., (Capt. late R.A.) 1/ 2/41
Delday, T.   1/ 2/41
Cruickshank, A.   1/ 2/41
Beveridge, J. K., M.C., (Capt.
late Can. Mil. Forces)   1/ 2/41
Lockhart, W., (2/Lt. late R.E.) 1/ 2/41

Lieutenants
Henderson, J.   1/ 2/41
Watson, A. E.   1/ 2/41
Mitchell, J.   1/ 2/41
Spence, J. R.   1/ 2/41
Paterson, H. (Capt. late
M.G. Corps)   1/ 2/41
Young, W.   1/ 2/41
Loney, A. (2/Lt. late Black
Watch)   1/ 2/41
Gibb, A.   1/ 2/41
Wardlaw, D.   1/ 2/41
Graham, M. T.   1/ 2/41

Lieutenants - contd.
Lawrence, L. A.   1/ 2/41
Hollingworth, L. A.   1/ 2/41
McCall, M. McI.   1/ 2/41
Dempsey, E.   1/ 2/41
Forrester, J.   1/ 2/41
Boyd, H. M.   1/ 2/41
Mackie, W. J.   1/ 2/41
Mitchell, W.   1/ 2/41
Boyter, H. R.   1/ 2/41
McArthur, R. B.   1/ 2/41
Cochran, W. M.   1/ 2/41

2nd Lieutenants
MacLean, H. M.   1/ 2/41
Turner, T. R.   1/ 2/41
Grieve, J. K.   1/ 2/41
Simpson, A.   1/ 2/41
Macdonald, R.   1/ 2/41
Thomas, W. R., (2/Lt. late
R.A.)   1/ 2/41
Swinfen, T. B.   1/ 2/41
Watson, W. N.   1/ 8/41

Adjutant & Quarter-Master
Plampin, Capt. (actg. 10/5/41)
W. H., Gen. List. Inf.   10/ 5/41

Medical Officer
Fleming, Maj. J. B., M.D.   1/ 2/41

54

6th FIFE BATTALION

Lt.-Colonel

Nicolson, H. S. (Lt. late
R.N.V.R.)   1/ 2/41

Majors

Cousin, W.   1/ 2/41
Paterson, A. (Lt. late Black
Watch)   1/ 2/41
Hunter, W.   1/ 2/41
Lindsay, W. S. (Capt. late
R.E.)   1/ 2/41
Rodger, J. B. (Lt. late M.G.
Corps)   1/ 2/41
Kay, J. W., (Capt. late
Gordons)   1/ 2/41
Hawthorn, W.   1/ 2/41

Captains

Robertson, A. L.   1/ 2/41
Scott, J.   1/ 2/41
Williamson, J. N.   1/ 2/41
Moyles, P., D.C.M., M.M.   1/ 2/41
Watson, A.   1/ 2/41
Soutar, J.   1/ 2/41

Lieutenants

Ford, G. W.   1/ 2/41
Mitchell, A. I.   1/ 2/41
Neilson, A., D.C.M., M.M.   1/ 2/41
Taylor, C. H.   1/ 2/41
Shaw, W.   1/ 2/41
Reid, W. (Lt. late T.A.)   1/ 2/41
Jarvis, P. R.   1/ 2/41
Peach, W. E. S.   1/ 2/41
Hodge, G. R. D., M.C. (2/Lt.
late Black Watch)   1/ 2/41

Lieutenants - contd.

Breen, J.   1/ 2/41
Reekie, A.   1/ 2/41
Pirie, J. W.   1/ 2/41
Farries, J.   1/ 2/41
Anderson, J. (Lt. late R.N.R.) 1/ 2/41
Penden, R. M.   1/ 2/41
Deas, D. W.   1/ 2/41
Nicoll, G. O.   1/ 2/41
Lyall, D. R.   1/ 2/41
Nisbet, A.   1/ 2/41
Robertson, W. Y. A. (Lt. late
R.E.)   1/ 2/41
Syme, J. W.   1/ 2/41
Brown, T.   1/ 2/41
Wemyss, W., M.M.   1/ 2/41
Patterson, A., D.C.M.   1/ 2/41
Reid, W.   1/ 2/41
Westwater, A.   1/ 2/41
Durie, D.   14/ 6/41
Jones, C.   19/ 7/41

2nd Lieutenants

Wylie, H.   1/ 2/41
Reid, J.   1/ 2/41

Adjutant & Quarter-Master

Dougary, Capt. (actg. 1/5/41)
J. G., Gen. List Inf.   1/ 5/41

Medical Officer

Stephen, Maj. A. (Lt. late
R.A.M.C.)   1/ 2/41

56455-3(36)

7th FIFE BATTALION

Lt.-Colonel	
Robertson, W. B. (Maj. late Serv. Bn., R. Scots)	1/ 2/41

Majors	
Hunt, R. H. A. (Lt. late T.A.)	1/ 2/41
Elder, A. J. (Capt. late T.A.)	1/ 2/41
Blair, R. M.	1/ 2/41
Miller, W. B.	1/ 2/41
Butler, J. D.	1/ 7/41

Captains	
Wilkie, J. (Capt. late M.C. Corps)	1/ 2/41
Tulloch, H. H.	1/ 2/41
Craig, W. H. (Capt. late A. & S.H.)	1/ 2/41
Mackay, W. J. (Lt. T.A. Res.)	1/ 2/41
Wightman, H. J.	1/ 7/41

Lieutenants	
Dickson, A. F.	1/ 2/41
Jackson, J. E.	1/ 2/41
Ferguson, J. M.	1/ 2/41
Gatherum, R. N.	1/ 2/41
Cole, P.	1/ 2/41
Donaldson, C. R.	1/ 2/41
Glancy, T.	1/ 2/41
Wailes, F. G. (Capt. late R.G.A.)	1/ 2/41
Kirk, H.	1/ 2/41
Stewart, C.	1/ 2/41
Wilson, E.	1/ 2/41
Barron, D. A.	1/ 2/41
Dawson, G. V.	1/ 2/41
Horne, T. S., M.M.	1/ 2/41
Orr, J. (Capt. late ... & S.H.)	1/ 2/41
Bibby, A.	1/ 2/41
Cape, J. D.	1/ 2/41
Anderson, L. H.	1/ 7/41
Hodge, H. F., M.C., T.D. (Maj. late T.A.)	10/ 7/41

2nd Lieutenants	
Wilson, J. F.	1/ 2/41
Todd, W. B.	1/ 2/41
Swan, J.	1/ 2/41
Hood, J. F. L.	1/ 2/41
Thomson, A.	1/ 2/41
Gardiner, R. P.	1/ 2/41
McQueen, J.	1/ 2/41
Miles, H.	1/ 2/41
Reid, T.	1/ 2/41
Cottrell, S.	1/ 2/41
Dalzell, E. A.	1/ 2/41
Brown, P.	1/ 2/41
McLennan, C.	1/ 2/41
Young, J. S.	1/ 2/41
Black, H.	1/ 2/41
Robertson, J. D.	1/ 2/41
Slavin, J.	1/ 2/41
Thomson, W.	1/ 2/41
Duncan, T.	1/ 2/41
Bald, R.	1/ 2/41
Speed, J. G.	1/ 2/41
Greig, W.	1/ 2/41
Bennett, W. (2/Lt. late R.A.F.)	1/ 2/41
Adamson, R.	1/ 2/41
Gilmour, H. M.	1/ 2/41
Dick, C. J. M.	1/ 2/41
Archibald, J.	1/ 2/41
Mills, J. D.	1/ 7/41
Martin, T.	1/ 7/41
Muirhead, A. J.	1/ 7/41
Bell, A. R.	1/ 7/41

Adjutant & Quarter-Master

Medical Officers	
Gumley, Maj. G. A. H.	1/ 2/41
Tuke, Capt., A. L. S., M.C., T.D. (Maj. late R.A.M.C.)	1/ 2/41

8th FIFE BATTALION

Lt.-Colonel	
Collyer, J. A. M., (Capt. late M.G. Corps)	1/ 2/41

Majors	
Beveridge, D., (Maj. late T.A.)	1/ 2/41
Herd, W., M.C., (Capt. late Black Watch)	1/ 2/41
Mickel, H. W.	1/ 2/41
Smith, P. W., (Lt. late R.A.F.)	1/ 2/41
Riddell, M. H.	1/ 2/41

Captains	
Mackay, A. R. (Lt. late Lincoln R.)	1/ 2/41
Stein, J.	1/ 2/41
McLeod, T. H.	1/ 2/41
Stewart, W. J.	1/ 2/41
Matthew, D. H.	1/ 2/41
Stewart, J., (Lt. late Black Watch)	1/ 2/41
Clark, G. (Lt. T.A. Res.)	1/ 2/41

Lieutenants	
Simpson, J. C., M.M.	1/ 2/41
Carr, J. C. B.	1/ 2/41
Carnegie, J. G.	1/ 2/41
Keddie, D. (Lt. late H.L.I.)	1/ 2/41
McGeachy, E., (Lt. late R.F.A.)	1/ 2/41

Lieutenants — contd.	
Marshall, C. H.	1/ 2/41
McLean, W.	1/ 2/41
Herning, F. J.	1/ 2/41
Bell, J. R.	1/ 2/41
Hare, A. T. S.	1/ 2/41
Millar, R. M.	1/ 2/41
Clark, R.	1/ 2/41
Logan, J.	1/ 2/41
Cheyne, A., (Lt. late Gordons)	15/ 7/41
Stocks, J., M.M.	17/ 7/41

2nd Lieutenants	
Ballantyne, F. D.	1/ 2/41
Ferguson, W. N., M.M.	1/ 2/41
Hutchison, R. S.	1/ 2/41
Montgomery, H.	1/ 2/41
Ross, J.	1/.2/41
Strachan, R.	1/ 2/41
Yeaman, R. D.	1/ 2/41
Westlands, W. H.	1/ 8/41

Adjutant & Quarter-Master

Medical Officer	
Hay, Maj. J. R. W., M.D.	1/ 2/41

9th FIFE BATTALION

Lt.-Colonel
Archibald, D. M., M.C., (Capt. late T.A.)   1/ 2/41

Majors
Todd, W. J. W.   1/ 2/41
Cook, G. E.   1/ 2/41
Guest, S. A.   1/ 2/41

Captains
Russell, J. W.   1/ 2/41
Goddard, L. J. E.   1/ 2/41
Coleman, H. F. W.   1/ 2/41
Nye, A.   1/ 2/41
Anderson, J. M.   1/ 2/41
Ranton, F. W.   1/ 2/41
Fergus, A. S.   1/ 2/41

Lieutenants
Scott, A.   1/ 2/41
Turner, T. S.   1/ 2/41
Gallacher, J.   1/ 2/41
Grimes, J. A.   1/ 2/41
Laurenson, A.   1/ 2/41
Campbell, H.   1/ 2/41
Castle-Smith, M. H. P.   1/ 2/41
Heath, R. G. G.   1/ 2/41
McCauley, H. R.   1/ 2/41
Gunn, D. S.   1/ 2/41
Hamilton, J.   1/ 2/41
Paton, G. S.   1/ 2/41
Sudweekes, W. H.   1/ 2/41
Lloyd, V. L.   1/ 2/41
Savage, C. H. N.   1/ 2/41
Pratt, A.   1/ 2/41
Greig, J.   1/ 2/41
Hutchison, J.   1/ 2/41
Browne, W. C.   1/ 2/41
Wilson, J. C.   1/ 2/41
Stewart, C.   1/ 2/41
Davidson, W. R.   1/ 2/41
Hutton, J. D. S.   1/ 2/41
King, J.   1/ 2/41
Edwards, B. W.   1/ 2/41
Martin, R. R.   1/ 2/41
McCauley, H. R., (2/Lt. late T.A.)   1/ 2/41

2nd Lieutenants

Adjutant & Quarter-Master

Medical Officer

DETACHED COMPANY KINROSS-SHIRE

Lt.-Colonel

Majors
Izat, W. R., D.S.O. (Lt.-Col. late R.E.)   1/ 2/41

Captains
Scott-Davidson, W. W. (Capt. late R.A.F.)   1/ 2/41

Lieutenants
Tullis, R.   1/ 2/41
Kirker, A. MacN.   1/ 2/41
Walker, T.   1/ 2/41

2nd Lieutenants
Young, D. R.   1/ 2/41
McCombe, J.   1/ 2/41
Sullivan, J. L.   1/ 2/41
Moncreiff, The Lord   5/ 7/41
Runcieman, J. W.   1/ 8/41

SOUTH HIGHLAND AREA - contd.

NO.4 ZONE (STIRLING & CLACKMANNANSHIRE)

Commander	Orr-Ewing, Col., Sir Norman A., Bt., D.S.O., (Hon. Brig.-Gen., ret. pay) (Col. ret. T.A.) 1/ 2/41
Second-in-Command	Bain, Lt.-Col., A. R., M.C., (Col. T.A.) 1/ 2/41
Territorial Army Association administering	The Stirling & Clackmannanshire T.A. Association, 12, Snowdon Place, Stirling.

1st STIRLINGSHIRE BATTALION

Lt-Colonel
Younger, The Visct., D.S.O., T.D.,
(Hon. Col. T.A.)   1/ 2/41

Majors
Walker, A., (Maj. late Camel
Corps)   1/ 2/41
Donaldson, N. P., C.B.E.   1/ 2/41
Stewart, W., C.B.E., (Maj.
ret.)   1/ 2/41
Young, K. M., (Maj. late T.A.)   1/ 2/41

Captains
Green, N. B., (Capt. late
R.W.K.)   1/ 2/41
Clark, J. (Capt. late H.L.I.)   1/ 2/41

Lieutenants
Sutherland J.   1/ 2/41
Starkey, R. K.   1/ 2/41
McEwan, D.   1/ 2/41
Sutherland, J. A.   1/ 2/41
Kitchin. J. B.   1/ 2/41
McAleese, J.   1/ 2/41
Kelly, J. A. (Lt. late
A. & S.H.)   1/ 2/41
Lunn, J. T.   1/ 2/41
Robertson, N. A.   1/ 2/41
Burns, J.   1/ 2/41
Orr, J. D.   1/ 2/41
Davidson, W. C., O.B.E.   1/ 2/41
McLaren, L. D.   1/ 2/41
Michie, J. T.   1/ 2/41
Ross, R. E. (Capt. late
Ind. Army)   1/ 2/41
Ritchie, T. C.   1/ 2/41

Lieutenants - contd.
McKechnie, D. (Capt. late
Gordons)   1/ 2/41
Williams, F. J. H.   1/ 2/41
Wilson, R. Y.
(Capt. T. A. Res.)   1/ 7/41

2nd Lieutenants
Pennycook, J.   1/ 2/41
Sutherland, J.   1/ 2/41
Coyle, J., M.M.   1/ 2/41
Irving, M.   1/ 2/41
Henderson, J. D. (Lt. late
R.F.A.)   1/ 2/41
Berguis, A. N. (Capt. late
R.F.A.)   1/ 2/41
Graham, J. O.   1/ 2/41
Drummond, W.   1/ 2/41
Dunsmore, A. C.   1/ 2/41
Burnett, R.   1/ 2/41
Adam, R. H.   18/ 7/41

Adjutant & Quarter-Master
Mitchell, Capt. (actg. 1/2/41)
W., Gen. List Inf.   1/ 2/41

Medical Officers
Wilson, Maj. J. W., M.B.
(Capt. late H.L.I.)   1/ 2/41
Stroyan, Capt. R. S. (Capt.
late R.A.)   1/ 2/41

2nd STIRLINGSHIRE BATTALION

Lt. -Colonel
Stein, A., M.C., T.D., (Col. T.A. Res.)   1/ 2/41

Majors
Haddow, R. T., M.C., (Maj. late R.A.)   1/ 2/41
White, J., (Lt. late Lan. Fus.) 1/ 2/41
Farrell, J. (2/Lt. late M.G. Corps.)   1/ 2/41
Macnair, R., (2/Lt. late Gds. M.G.R.)   1/ 2/41
Sharp, A.   1/ 2/41

Captains
Armstrong, H., M.M.   1/ 2/41
Davie, H. C., M.C. (Lt. late Camerons)   1/ 2/41
Curran, J. F., D.C.M., M.M.   1/ 2/41
Thomson, A. E. (Lt. late D.L.I.)   1/ 2/41

Lieutenants
Brown, J. S.   1/ 2/41
Harvey, R., D.C.M., M.M.   1/ 2/41
Hill, J.   1/ 2/41
Mathieson, C. W.   1/ 2/41
Rattray, W. C., M.C. (Lt. late R.F.A.)   1/ 2/41
Thomson, R. H., M.M. (2/Lt. late Gordons)   1/ 2/41
Brown, R. M. W. (2/Lt. late R.F.A.)   1/ 2/41
Wortley, G. W.   1/ 2/41
Green, J.   1/ 2/41

Lieutenants - contd.
Moore, J. C.   1/ 2/41
Barlow, H.   1/ 2/41
McLaren, A., M.M.   1/ 2/41
Haston, M. D.   1/ 2/41
Johnston, A.   1/ 2/41
Pryde, J., M.M.   1/ 2/41
Boston, E. J.   1/ 2/41
Wilson, R.   1/ 2/41
Hossack, J. D.   1/ 2/41
Monfries, J. W.   1/ 2/41
Fraser, T.   1/ 2/41
Riddell, H. W.   1/ 2/41
Turnbull, R. S.   1/ 2/41
Roger, J.   1/ 2/41
McCowan, R. R.   1/ 2/41
Grierson, J.   1/ 2/41
Millar, J. M.   1/ 2/41
Ewen, G. T.   1/ 2/41
McAlpine, D.   1/ 2/41

2nd Lieutenants
McEwan, W.   1/ 2/41
Lawson, A. C.   1/ 2/41

Adjutant & Quarter-Master

Medical Officer
McLachlan, Maj., D. C., T.D., (Lt.-Col. late R.A.M.C.)   1/ 2/41

63

3rd STIRLINGSHIRE BATTALION

Lt.-Colonel
Thomson, J. J. S., M.C.,
(Capt. late T.A.)   1/ 2/41

Majors
Peddie, R. B., M.C. (Capt.
late T.A.)   1/ 2/41
Tough, D.   1/ 2/41
Paterson, J.   1/ 2/41
Wilson, A. W. (2/Lt. late
R. Scots)   1/ 2/41
Edmond, W. (2/Lt. late
A. & S.H.)   1/ 2/41
Thompson, J.S. (Lt. Res.
of Off.)   1/ 2/41

Captains
McKinley, D.   1/ 2/41
McBryde, W.   1/ 2/41
Webb, B. W., (Sub/Lt. late
R.N.V.R.)   1/ 2/41
McLaren, J., (Lt. late
A. & S.H.)   1/ 2/41
Griffiths, F. G., (Lt. late
A. & S.H.)   1/ 2/41
Davies, T.I., (Capt. late
Welch R.)   1/ 2/41

Lieutenants
Etchells, K. K.   1/ 2/41
Macintyre, D., M.M.   1/ 2/41
Boyd, G. C. H.   1/ 2/41
Shanks, W. M.   1/ 2/41
Campbell, D. B.,   1/ 2/41
Peddie, R. M., (2/Lt. late
R.F.A.)   1/ 2/41
Moodie, A. J., M.M.   1/ 2/41
Nelson, J. K.   1/ 2/41
Galbraith, J.   1/ 2/41
Hay, A.   1/ 2/41
Malcolm, T. J.   1/ 2/41
Muir, W.   1/ 2/41

Lieutenants - contd.
Macfarlane, E. O., (Capt.
late Midd'x. R.)   1/ 2/41
Atkinson, A. W.   1/ 2/41
Forrester, A. F. C.   1/ 2/41
Chalmers, J. B.   1/ 2/41
Sanderson, W. N.   1/ 2/41
Hannigan, J.   1/ 2/41
Watt, A.   1/ 2/41
Bain, W., (2/Lt. late T.A.)   1/ 2/41
Liddell, P.   1/ 2/41
Brisbane, R. S.   1/ 2/41
Greig, R.   1/ 2/41

2nd Lieutenants
Thomson, J. C.   1/ 2/41
Stanners, G. C.   1/ 2/41
Glen, J. P.   1/ 2/41
Abercrombie, C.   1/ 2/41
Bryson, J. K.   1/ 2/41
Johnson, J.   1/ 2/41
Elmslie, V. G.   1/ 2/41
Graham, W., M.M.   1/ 2/41
Whitehead, W.   1/ 2/41
Carruthers, R.   1/ 2/41
Stewart, J. C.   1/ 2/41
Christine, J.   1/ 2/41
Stanners, T. W.   1/ 2/41
McArthur, J.   1/ 2/41
Forsyth, W. R.   1/ 2/41
Polley, J.   1/ 2/41
Bauchop, J. A. (2/Lt. late
R.A.F.)   1/ 2/41

Adjutant & Quarter-Master

Medical Officer
King, Maj., H. McK., M.B.   1/ 2/41

1st CLACKMANNANSHIRE BATTALION

Lt.-Colonel			**Lieutenants - contd.**	
Spens, H. B., D.S.O., T.D.,		Simpson, E., (Capt. late	
(Col. T.A.)	1/ 2/41	Gordons)	1/ 2/41
		Lambert, J. A.	1/ 2/41
		Dickie, R.	1/ 2/41
		Allan, J.	1/ 2/41
		Dick, J.	1/ 2/41
		Dawson, J. (Lt. late	
		A. & S.H.)	1/ 2/41
Majors		Burnett, D. McG. (Capt. T.A.	
Tullis, J. K., (Maj. late		Res.)	1/ 2/41
A. & S.H.)	1/ 2/41	Kinross, W. C. (2/Lt. late	
Brotherton, J. B., (Capt.		Gordons)	1/ 2/41
late Ind. Army)	1/ 2/41	Buchanan, W.	1/ 2/41
Jardine, J., (Lt. late T.A.)	1/ 2/41	Le Fanu. J. L.	1/ 2/41
McIntyre, R. B., (Lt. late		Strang, T. W.	1/ 2/41
Gordons)	1/ 2/41		
Whitson, R. S., M.C., (Capt.			
late R. Scots)	1/ 2/41		
		2nd Lieutenants	
		Mitchell, R.	1/ 2/41
		Turner, T. W.	25/ 7/41
Captains			
White, J. B.	1/ 2/41		
Rintoul, A. Y.	1/ 2/41		
Cunningham, G. F.	1/ 2/41		
Anderson, A.	1/ 2/41		
		Adjutant & Quarter-Master	
Lieutenants			
Manzies, R. W.	1/ 2/41		
Foggo, A.	1/ 2/41		
Douglas, J. F.	1/ 2/41	**Medical Officer**	
Atchley, K. W.	1/ 2/41	Faulkner, Capt. W. E.	1/ 2/41
Kirkwood, T. W., M.M.,			
(2/Lt. late M.G. Corps)	1/ 2/41		
Barn, J.	1/ 2/41		
Gray, R. C.	1/ 2/41		
Scott, J.	1/ 2/41		

SOUTH HIGHLAND AREA - contd.

NO.5 ZONE (NORTH ARGYLL)

Commander	Hall, Col., Sir Douglas M. B., Bt., D.S.O., (Lt.-Col. ret. pay) (Res. of Off.) 1/ 2/41
Engineer Officer	Macdougall of Macdougall, Capt., A. J., C.M.G., (Col. late R.A.M.C.) 1/ 2/41
Medical Officer	Macnicol, Maj. R. R., M.B. 24/ 6/41
Territorial Army Association administering	County of Argyll T.A. Association, The Drill Hall, Dunoon.

1st ARGYLL (NORTH) BATTALION

Colonel

Hall, Sir Douglas M. B., Bt., D.S.O. (Lt.-Col. ret. pay) (Res. of Off.) 1/ 2/41

Majors

Cooper, H. A., (Maj. ret.) 1/ 2/41
Fletcher, A. M., (Maj. late Camerons) 1/ 2/41
Blakeney, H. E. H., M.C., (Capt. late R. Sussex R.) 1/ 2/41
Cuninghame, R. D. S., (Capt. late S. Gds.) 1/ 2/41
Graeme, N. F., (Lt.-Col. late Ind. Army) 1/ 2/41
Mellor, J. G. G., M.C. (Maj. late K.R.R.C.) 1/ 2/41
Methuen, Hon. L. P., (Lt. Res. of Off.) 1/ 2/41

Captains

Macdonald, R. C. 1/ 2/41
Dalgleish, J. P. (Lt. late T.A.) 1/ 2/41
Lang, G. W. 1/ 2/41
Disselduff, J., M.C. (Capt. late A. & S.H.) 1/ 2/41
Ainsworth, Sir Thomas, Bt., (Lt. late 11th H.) 1/ 2/41
Macqueen, R. H., C.B.E. (Maj. late R.A.S.C.) 1/ 2/41

Lieutenants

MacLean, J. 1/ 2/41
Munro, N. M. 1/ 2/41
Yorworth, F. J. 1/ 2/41
Edgar, R. W. 1/ 2/41
Campbell, J. D., (Lt. late The King's R.) 1/ 2/41
Stewart of Coll, E. M. P., C.B., C.B.E., (Col. late R.E.) 1/ 2/41

Lieutenants - contd.

Campbell-Baldwin, R. H., D.S.O. (Lt.-Col. late E. Surrey R.) 1/ 2/41
Dunn, H. 1/ 2/41
Banks, J. H. 1/ 2/41
Mathieson, J. G., (Lt. late A. & S.H.) 1/ 2/41
Pawson, W. H., (Capt. ret.) 1/ 2/41
Rae, W. L. 1/ 2/41
Macdonald, W. 1/ 2/41
Watson, J. A. 7/ 6/41
MacLaren, I. 7/ 6/41
Barbour, M. H. 20/ 6/41
Gargan, R. (Lt. late A. & S.H.) 7/ 7/41

2nd Lieutenants

Carter, H. 1/ 2/41
Macisaac, G. W., M.M. 1/ 2/41
Mackenzie, M. 1/ 2/41
May, D. 1/ 2/41
Campbell, A., (Maj. ret.) 1/ 2/41
Stevenson, I. T., O.B.E., (Lt. late R.N.V.R.) 1/ 2/41
Macphee, A. 1/ 2/41
McAlpin, J. D. 1/ 2/41
Dudgeon, W. C. (Lt. late R.G.A.) 1/ 2/41
Macdonald, R. N., (2/Lt. late T.A.) 1/ 2/41
Colyer-Fergusson, W. P., (2/Lt. late North'n. R.) 1/ 2/41
Nelson, T. E. 1/ 2/41
Graham, J. 1/ 2/41
McIntyre, A. B. 18/ 6/41
McKenzie, A. 5/ 7/41

Adjutant & Quarter-Master

Medical Officer

EDINBURGH AREA

General Staff Officer 1st grade	Grant-Suttie, Col. H. F., D.S.O., M.C., ret. pay (Res. of Off.) p.s.c≠.,n.s. 1/ 7/40

CITY OF EDINBURGH ZONE

Commander	Drummond, Col. W. M.C., (Capt. late Gordons)	1/ 2/41
Second-in-Command	Cameron, Lt.-Col. N. J. G., C.B., C.M.G., (Maj.-Gen. ret. pay)	1/ 2/41
Assistant to Commander	Reid, Maj. R. (Lt. late T.A.)	1/ 2/41
	Morrison, Capt. H. P., M.C., (Maj. late R.r'.A.)	1/ 2/41
Staff Officer	Reid, Capt. R. A.	1/ 2/41
Weapon Training Officer	Campbell, Capt. C. D. M. (2/Lt. T.A. Res.)	1/ 2/41
Chief Guide	Lambert, Capt. J. (Maj. late T.A.)	1/ 2/41
Intelligence Officer	Thomson, Capt. W. T., M.C., (Capt. late A. & S. H.)	1/ 2/41
Liaison Officer	Oliver, Capt. Sir Arthur, C.B., C.M.G., (Col. late R.A.V.C.)	1/ 2/41
Signal Officer	Hepburn, Capt. E. J. (Capt. late R.A.O.C.)	1/ 2/41
Assistant Signal Officer	Gaunt, Lt., T.	1/ 2/41
Transport Officer	Harrower, Lt. W. P.	1/ 2/41
Territorial Army Association ⎫ administering ⎬	City of Edinburgh T.A. Association, 19, Palmerston Place, Edinburgh.	

1st CITY OF EDINBURGH BATTALION

Lt.-Colonel

Foulis, D. A., D.S.O., (Lt.-Col. late Serv. Bn. Sco. Re≠.)	1/ 2/41

Majors

Bell, J. C., M.C., (Maj. T.A. Res.)	1/ 2/41
Ferguson, A. E., D.C.M.	1/ 2/41
Hicks, A. A.	1/ 2/41
Lindsay, R. S., M.C., (Capt. late R. Scots)	1/ 2/41
Simpson, A.	1/ 2/41
Tulloch, D. (Capt. late Ind. Army)	1/ 2/41
Wighton, A. A. (Capt. late R.F.A.)	1/ 2/41
Young, J., M.C., (Capt. late R.Scots.)	1/ 2/41

Captains

Beattie, Y. H. (Capt. late T.A.)	1/ 2/41
Bryce, S. M. (Capt. late Labour Corps)	1/ 2/41
Crichton, A. D. (Lt. late Ind. Army)	1/ 2/41
Currie, J. (Lt. late Gordons)	1/ 2/41
Gorrie, R. L. (Capt. late R.Scots.)	1/ 2/41
Hendry, W. (Capt. late R.Ir.R.)	1/ 2/41
MacKean, P. K.	1/ 2/41
Weir, R. Y., O.B.E. (Maj. late T.A.)	1/ 2/41
Clark, Sir Thomas, Bt., (Maj. late R.Scots.)	1/ 2/41

Lieutenants

Andrews, G. H., (Lt. late R.Mar.)	1/ 2/41
Barrington, C. J.	1/ 2/41
Dunstall, W. L. P., M.C., (Capt. late R. Fus.)	1/ 2/41
Halliday, A.	1/ 2/41
Harvey, G. T. (Maj. late R.Scots.)	1/ 2/41
Kerr, H. N.	1/ 2/41
Lawrie, N. B.	1/ 2/41
Langdon, J. C.	1/ 2/41
Linnell, J. M.	1/ 2/41

Lieutenants - contd.

Little, R., M.M.	1/ 2/41
Munro, D.	1/ 2/41
Murray, W. (Lt. late R.G.A.)	1/ 2/41
Perkins, T.S. (2/Lt. late R.T.R.)	1/ 2/41
Salvesen, H. K. (Capt. late Ind. Army)	1/ 2/41
Shaw, W. D., M.C., (Maj. late H.L.I.)	1/ 2/41
Smart, R. M.	1/ 2/41
Swan, W. L. (Lt. late R.G.A.)	1/ 2/41
Terris, J.	1/ 2/41
Wallace, G. A. (Lt. late K.R.R.C.)	1/ 2/41
Gregor, D. H.	1/ 2/41
Patrick, J. C. (Capt. late R.Scots.)	1/ 2/41
Robertson, A. D.	1/ 2/41
Scott, A.	1/ 2/41

2nd Lieutenants

Adam, J. C.	1/ 2/41
Aitken, W. B.	1/ 2/41
Borthwick, W.	1/ 2/41
Cameron, J. E.	1/ 2/41
Gibson, F. R.	1/ 2/41
Hunter, H. B.	1/ 2/41
McLean, A. J. (2/Lt. late Gordons)	1/ 2/41
Menzies, D. F.	1/ 2/41
Rhodes, F. A. (Capt. late R.A.F.)	1/ 2/41
Urquhart, E. A.	1/ 2/41
McKechnie, J.	5/ 7/41

Adjutant & Quarter-Master

Neilson, Capt. (act≠ 15/5/41) I.B.C., Gen. List Inf.	15/ 5/41

Medical Officer

Bailey, Maj. R., M.B.	1/ 2/41

EDINBURGH AREA - contd.

CITY OF EDINBURGH ZONE - contd.

2nd CITY OF EDINBURGH BATTALION

Lt.-Colonel

Strang, J. L., (Maj. late M.G. Corps)	1/ 2/41

Majors

Gem, W. H., (Capt. late M.G. Corps)	1/ 2/41
Allan, J. K., (Lt. late Gordons)	1/ 2/41
Fleming, R., (Capt. late M.G. Corps)	1/ 2/41
Howden, H., (Lt.-Col. late R.A.)	1/ 2/41
Mackenzie, A. D., O.B.E., (Maj. late R.E.)	1/ 2/41
Murray, J., (Capt. late Camerons)	1/ 2/41
Murray, R. F.	1/ 2/41
Tweedie, C. E.	1/ 2/41
Wylie, A. W., M.C., (Capt. late K.O.S.B.)	1/ 2/41
Black, C., (Lt. late R.A.F.)	27/ 6/41

Captains

Edwards, J. T.	1/ 2/41
Hamilton, F.	1/ 2/41
McAllister, D., M.M.	1/ 2/41
McGregor, C. G.	1/ 2/41
Matley, C. S., (Capt. late T.A.)	1/ 2/41
Sharp, T. S., (2/Lt. late R. Scots)	1/ 2/41
Stoddart, W. L., (Lt. late Labour Corps)	1/ 2/41
Williamson, H. R. (Capt. late T.A.)	1/ 2/41
Nichols, J. E., (2/Lt. late T.A.)	1/ 2/41

Lieutenants

Burnett, J.	1/ 2/41
Campbell, W., (2/Lt. late H.L.I.)	1/ 2/41
Bruce, R., M.C., (Maj. late R.E.)	1/ 2/41
Cowe, A. S.	1/ 2/41
Dunbar, P. J.	1/ 2/41
Edward, J. C.	1/ 2/41
Gordon, P. S.	1/ 2/41
Grant, J.	1/ 2/41
Heron, J. E.	1/ 2/41
Illingworth, R. E.	1/ 2/41
Hogg, R. R.	1/ 2/41
McDonald, J. R.	1/ 2/41
McNaughton, T.	1/ 2/41
McNulty, J., (Lt. late K.O.S.B.)	1/ 2/41
Middleton, J. T.	1/ 2/41
Milne, F. J.	1/ 2/41
Muirhead, J. A.	1/ 2/41
Ogilvy, N. J., (Lt. late R. Scots.)	1/ 2/41
Rae, R., (Lt. late Surrey R.)	1/ 2/41

Lieutenants - contd.

Ritchie, A. W., (2/Lt. late R. Fus.)	1/ 2/41
Smith, J. J., (2/Lt. late R.G.A.)	1/ 2/41
Spankie, G.	1/ 2/41
Stevenson, M., M.C.	1/ 2/41
Thomson, W. H.	1/ 2/41
Wallace, C. F.	1/ 2/41
Wotherspoon, J. W., (Lt. late Cameronians)	1/ 2/41
Wylie, R.	1/ 2/41
Glendinning, S.	1/ 6/41
Laurie, J. H., M.M.	1/ 6/41
Lunn, W. C.	17/ 7/41

2nd Lieutenants

Alexander, G.	1/ 2/41
Allan, M.	1/ 2/41
Ames, W. M., (Lt. late Black Watch)	1/ 2/41
Campbell, W. G.	1/ 2/41
Ford, H. A. M.	1/ 2/41
Gilchrist, J.	1/ 2/41
Henderson, J. (2/Lt. late R. Scots)	1/ 2/41
Henderson, J.	1/ 2/41
Howie, T. M.	1/ 2/41
Kelly, M. B.	1/ 2/41
Lindsay, J. T., (Capt. late Can. Mil. Forces)	1/ 2/41
Macfarlane, R.	1/ 2/41
Mackenzie, R. S.	1/ 2/41
MacQueen, C.	1/ 2/41
Robertson, J.	1/ 2/41
Robson, J.	1/ 2/41
Stark, A. R., (Lt. late Seaforth)	1/ 2/41
Stewart, P. D.	1/ 2/41
Walter, R. C.	1/ 2/41
Laing, G. A.	1/ 2/41
Godfrey, T.	1/ 2/41
Campbell, D. E. (2/Lt. late A. & S.H.)	27/ 6/41
Wylie, T.	1/ 7/41
Cheyne, J. A.	18/ 7/41

Adjutant & Quarter-Master

McGill, Capt. (actg. 28/5/41) A. S., Gen. List Inf.	28/ 5/41

Medical Officer

Robb, Maj. A. P. (late Surgeon/Lt. R.N.)	1/ 2/41

3rd CITY OF EDINBURGH BATTALION

Lt.-Colonel
Ker, R. F., D.S.O., M.C.,
(Lt.-Col. late K.O.S.B.)   1/ 2/41

Majors
Atkins, W. J., (Capt.
late R.F.A.)   1/ 2/41
Morhan, J., (Maj. late R.A.M.C.)   1/ 2/41
Cameron, W. M., M.B.E.,
(Capt. late Seaforth)   1/ 2/41
Cray, A. F., M.C., (Capt.
late T.A.)   1/ 2/41
Hampton, T., (Lt. late
M.G. Corps)   1/ 2/41
Haynes, W. F., (Lt.-Col. late
Ind. Army)   1/ 2/41
McGregor, D. G., A.F.C.,
(Capt. late R.A.F.)   1/ 2/41
Pullen, E. W., (Lt. late
London R.)   1/ 2/41
Stewart, G. O., (Lt. late
Ind. Army)   1/ 2/41
Stirling, C. F., M.B.E.,
(Lt. late Gloster R.)   1/ 2/41
White, A. L., (Lt. late R.N.R.) 1/ 2/41

Captains
Brownlie, J. R., M.C., (Capt.
late Border R.)   1/ 2/41
Forbes, A.I.   1/ 2/41
Forbes, E. S., (Lt. late R.A.)   1/ 2/41
Hillard, F.   1/ 2/41
Jamieson, R., (Lt. late
Rifle Bde.)   1/ 2/41
Kay, A., M.C., (Capt. late
K.O.S.B.)   1/ 2/41
McCulloch, J., M.M.   1/ 2/41
Philip, D., (Lt. late Border R.) 1/ 2/41
Rutherford, P.   1/ 2/41
Stevenson, W. H.   1/ 2/41
Watson, J. A., D.C.M., M.M.   1/ 2/41
Westwood, J. S., (Lt. late
Gordons)   1/ 2/41

Lieutenants
Martin, G. L.   1/ 2/41
Berry, W.   1/ 2/41
Cave, A. W., M.C., (Capt.
late R.A.O.C.)   1/ 2/41
Cleghorn, J. F.   1/ 2/41
Cowe, S. T.   1/ 2/41
Crooke, W. P.   1/ 2/41
Dickie, G. H., (Lt. late
K.O.S.B.)   1/ 2/41
Edgar, W., (Capt. late K.A.
Rif.)   1/ 2/41
Farmer, B. H., (Capt. late Oxf.
& Bucks. L.I.)   1/ 2/41
Finlay, D.   1/ 2/41
Gibson, T., (Capt. late R.T.R.) 1/ 2/41
Gillespie, W. D., M.C.,
(Capt. late R.Scots.)   1/ 2/41
Hatch, G. S., (Lt. late E.
Surrey R.)   1/ 2/41
Holman, H. H.   1/ 2/41
Kay, J., (Maj. late R.A.S.C.)   1/ 2/41
Kirkpatrick, G. W.   1/ 2/41
Mackay, J. B. I., (Lt. late
Nigeria R.)   1/ 2/41
Marshall, W. A.   1/ 2/41
McPherson, T. E.   1/ 2/41
Murdie, J.   1/ 2/41
Murphy, S. W., (Lt. late
R.A.S.C.)   1/ 2/41
Murray, D., D.C.M.   1/ 2/41
Ramsay, N. A. I.   1/ 2/41
Rarkin, J. G., (Lt. late
K.A. Rif.)   1/ 2/41
Rhind, C. O., (Lt. late
K.O.S.B.)   1/ 2/41
Robertson, J. F., (Capt.
late R.G.A.)   1/ 2/41
Ross, A.   1/ 2/41
Ross, J., (Capt. late
A. & S.H.)   1/ 2/41
St. Clair, S. F.   1/ 2/41
Sangster, L.   1/ 2/41
Simpson, R. F., (Lt. late
Gordons)   1/ 2/41
Sutherland, A. T.   1/ 2/41

3rd City of Edinburgh Battalion – contd.

Lieutenants – contd.			2nd Lieutenants – contd.		
Thomson, A.	1/ 2/41		Forbes, J.	16/ 6/41	
White, W.	1/ 2/41		Round, R. E.	16/ 6/41	
Winton, R. D.	1/ 2/41		Fleming, Lord, M.C. (Maj.		
Miller, J. (Lt. late			late.Inniskilling Fus.)	16/ 6/41	
(Cameronians)	9/ 6/41		Hall, J.	30/ 7/41	
Reid, W. D., (Capt. late R.E.)	14/ 6/41				
Penman, J.	22/ 7/41				

2nd Lieutenants

Allan, R.	1/ 2/41
Arnot, J.	1/ 2/41
Baird, D.	1/ 2/41
Brown, J. W.	1/ 2/41
Campbell, J.	1/ 2/41
Dow, G. T.	1/ 2/41
Douglas, J.	1/ 2/41
Duncan, J. F.	1/ 2/41
Elder, J., (Lt. late K.O.S.B.)	1/ 2/41
Garside, J. S.	1/ 2/41
Gemmell, J. G.	1/ 2/41
Girvan, A. D., (2/Lt. late	
R.S. Fus.)	1/ 2/41
Gray, G. B. R.	1/ 2/41
Gristwood, F. C.	1/ 2/41
Hunter, G. F.	1/ 2/41
Keir, D. R., D.S.O., (Lt.–	
Col. late Black Watch)	1/ 2/41
Meikle, J.	1/ 2/41
Purves, R. W.	1/ 2/41
Ritchie, M.	1/ 2/41
Sangster, G.	1/ 2/41
Simpson, J. G.	1/ 2/41
Thomson, J. F.	1/ 2/41
Walker, P.	1/ 2/41
Wallace, W., M.M.	1/ 2/41

Adjutant & Quarter-Master

Medical Officers

Morison, Maj. J., C.I.E., (Lt.–	
Col. late Ind. Med. Serv.)	1/ 2/41
Proudfoot, Capt. R., M.D.,	
(Maj. late R.A.M.C.)	18/ 7/41

56455-3(48)

4th CITY OF EDINBURGH BATTALION

Lt.-Colonel		
Blyth, B. H., (Lt.-Col. late R.E.)	1/ 2/41	

Captains — contd.		
Pearson, J.	1/ 2/41
Philip, G. G.	1/ 2/41
Rankin, D. B.	1/ 2/41
Robson, S.	1/ 2/41
Somerville, A. P.	14/ 5/41

Majors		
Gilderdale, H. A., (Capt. late R.E.)	1/ 2/41
Baird, W. J. S., M.C., (Maj. late R.A.)	1/ 2/41
Howes, H. W., (F/O late R.A.F.)	1/ 2/41
Law, F. H.	1/ 2/41
Lawson, W. D., (Maj. late M.G. Corps.)	1/ 2/41
McGregor, J., (Capt. late A. & S.H.)	1/ 2/41
Matthew, D. H., (Lt. late K.O.S.B.)	1/ 2/41
Morgan, T. L., (Maj. late R.E.)	1/ 2/41
Smith, J. R. L., (Lt. late R. Scots.)	1/ 2/41

Lieutenants		
Hagen, J.	1/ 2/41
Bisset, A. J.	1/ 2/41
Brisco, W. J. T.	1/ 2/41
Brown, W. A.	1/ 2/41
Collins, W. R.	1/ 2/41
Cook, C. A.	1/ 2/41
Coull, J.	1/ 2/41
Crocket, A. B.	1/ 2/41
Douglas, F. T. D.	1/ 2/41
Duff, D.	1/ 2/41
Faichney, T. J. McL.	1/ 2/41
Galloway, J. F., (Capt. late R.E.)	1/ 2/41
Ford, G.	1/ 2/41
Goodall, W.	1/ 2/41
Graham, A.	1/ 2/41
Gunn, G.	1/ 2/41
Harcus, F. W.	1/ 2/41
Hislop, A. D.	1/ 2/41
Hoy, J. L., (Lt. late R.Scots.)	1/ 2/41
Hunter, J. P.	1/ 2/41
Kirkpatrick, W. G. L.	1/ 2/41
Makon, J. McC., M.M.	1/ 2/41
McAlpine, R. R.	1/ 2/41
Mackinnon, J.	1/ 2/41
Mathie, K.	1/ 2/41
Mort, W. R.	1/ 2/41
Muir, R. F.	1/ 2/41
Reid, J. H.	1/ 2/41
Rodger, W. M.	1/ 2/41

Captains		
Eccles, J. (2/Lt. late R.A.)	1/ 2/41
Angus, J., (Lt. late Gordons)	1/ 2/41
Benzies, J.	1/ 2/41
Broughton, T. N.	1/ 2/41
Cross, H. J., M.M., (2/Lt. late H.L.I.)	1/ 2/41
Ferguson, W., (Lt. late H.L.I.)	1/ 2/41
Haldane, D., (Lt. late R. Scots.)	1/ 2/41

74

4th City of Edinburgh Battalion - contd.

Lieutenants - contd.

Routledge, F. R.	1/ 2/41
Sinclair, D., (Lt. late T.A.)	1/ 2/41
Stevens, A. W.	1/ 2/41
Simpton, R.	1/ 2/41
Weir, A. J., M.M.	1/ 2/41
Densem, N. E.	1/ 2/41
Geddes, R., (Lt. late R.F.A.)	1/ 2/41
Macdiarmid, E., (Lt. T.A. Res.)	1/ 2/41
Macgregor, I. P., (Capt. late Cameronians)	1/ 2/41
Cresser, C.	1/ 6/41
Pond, L. J.	1/ 6/41
Shepherd, J.	23/ 6/41

2nd Lieutenants - contd.

Rose, C. A., M.C., (Capt. late R.F.A.)	1/ 2/41
Seymour, F.	1/ 2/41
Smith, V. H.	1/ 2/41
Stowell, P. D.	1/ 2/41
Walker, G. B.	1/ 2/41
Weddell, A.C.	1/ 2/41
Welsh, J.	1/ 2/41
Scott, R.	1/ 2/41
Spreckley, H. G.	1/ 2/41
Fisken, C.	1/ 2/41
McGechie, J. S.	23/ 6/41

2nd Lieutenants

Brown, G. K., (2/Lt. late R.G.A.)	1/ 2/41
Carrothers, C. G., (2/Lt. late R.E.)	1/ 2/41
Cloke, H. W. B.	1/ 2/41
Coghill, W. J.	1/ 2/41
Dalrymple, Sir Charles M., Bt. (Lt. late R.A.)	1/ 2/41
Dickson, A.	1/ 2/41
George, G. R.	1/ 2/41
Holmes, J.	1/ 2/41
Hunt, H. R., (Capt. late Can. Mil. Forces)	1/ 2/41
Hunt, T.	1/ 2/41
Kerr, J.	1/ 2/41
Liddle, H. W.	1/ 2/41
Miller, J. S. B.	1/ 2/41
Morris, A. A., (Lt. late R. North'd Fus.)	1/ 2/41
Paterson, J.	1/ 2/41
Ramsay, R. G.	1/ 2/41
Robertson, A.	1/ 2/41

Adjutant & Quarter-Master
Brown, Capt. (actg. 1/2/41)
J. A., V.D., Gen. List Inf.	1/ 2/41

Medical Officers
Callam, Maj. W.D.A., M.B., F.R.C.S.	1/ 2/41
Fisher, Maj. E. F., (Surgeon/ Lt. ret. R.N.)	1/ 7/41
Ferguson, Capt., P. J. K., M.B.	7/ 8/41

5th CITY OF EDINBURGH BATTALION

Lt.-Colonel

Reid, R. S., T.D., (Col.
ret. T.A.)   1/ 2/41

Captains - contd.

Rodger, J. W.	21/ 7/41
Robb, H.	21/ 7/41
White, W. (Capt. late	
M.G. Corps)	21/ 7/41
Reynolds, T.	21/ 7/41

Majors

Hanna, W. G. C., O.B.E.,	
(Capt. late T.A.)	1/ 2/41
Bastow, J. E.	1/ 2/41
Beaton, A., M.B.E., (Lt.	
late T.A.)	1/ 2/41
Gerrard, W. D., D.S.O., (Maj.	
late T.A.)	1/ 2/41
Guthrie, H. L. C., (Maj.	
late M.G. Corps.)	1/ 2/41
Johnston, G.	1/ 2/41
Sinclair, D. (Lt. late R.F.A.)	1/ 2/41
McCall, D., M.B.E.	21/ 7/41
Blight, E. W.	21/ 7/41

Lieutenants

Carlsson, G. E.	1/ 2/41
Clark, C. A.	1/ 2/41
Cleland, T., (Lt. late	
M.G. Corps.)	1/ 2/41
Cramb, G. E.	1/ 2/41
Cumming, D. W. C.	1/ 2/41
Edgar, R.	1/ 2/41
Gaunt, J., (Lt. late R.S. Fus.)	1/ 2/41
Grant, D. L.	1/ 2/41
Holroyd, C. W., (Lt. late	
A. & S.H.)	1/ 2/41
Laidlaw, J. D., (Maj. late	
R.E.)	1/ 2/41
Lawson, J.	1/ 2/41
Ovens, R. F.	1/ 2/41
Patten, W.	1/ 2/41
Primrose, W.	1/ 2/41
Reid, G.	1/ 2/41
Richards, A. B.	1/ 2/41
Rutherford, W.	1/ 2/41
Scott, J. H.	1/ 2/41
Smith, W.	1/ 2/41

Captains

Brechin, M., M.C., (Capt.	
late R.A.)	1/ 2/41
Johnstone, T., (Lt. late	
R.S. Fus.)	1/ 2/41
Nicholson, M. D.	1/ 2/41
Westwater, L. A., (Lt. late	
R. Scots.)	1/ 2/41
Richardson, R. L. T., M.C.,	
(Capt. late R. Scots)	14/ 5/41
Fyfe, J. S.	21/ 7/41
Down, S. G.	21/ 7/41

Sneddon, D.	1/ 2/41
Wighton, W. A.	1/ 2/41
Wilson, W.	1/ 2/41
Douglas, A. R.	1/ 6/41
Rodger, D., (2/Lt. late	
R.A.F.)	1/ 6/41
Reid, C. T.	18/ 6/41
Wallace, W. J.	21/ 7/41
Reid, J. D.	21/ 7/41
Mackenzie, J.	21/ 7/41

75a

5th City of Edinburgh Battalion - contd.

Lieutenants - contd.

Reid, W. McK.	21/ 7/41
Weir, T. (Lt. late K.O.S.B.)	21/ 7/41
Lamb, H. H., M.C. (Lt. late R.S. Fus.)	21/ 7/41
Gallie, R. A., M.C. (Capt. late T.A.)	21/ 7/41
Fraser, G. M. J.	21/ 7/41
Wood, G. A.	21/ 7/41
McDonald, W. C.	21/ 7/41
Dalgleish, D. N.	21/ 7/41
Jenkins, W.	21/ 7/41
Lindsay, W. C. S., M.C., (Maj. late R. Scots.)	21/ 7/41
Corstorphin, P.	21/ 7/41
Geddes, J.	21/ 7/41

2nd Lieutenants - contd.

Couzens, J. H.	21/ 7/41
Barclay, G. R.	21/ 7/41
Wilson, J. P. G.	21/ 7/41
Paterson, J.	21/ 7/41
Currie, J. D. M.	21/ 7/41
Ivory, E. J.	21/ 7/41
Muir, W.	21/ 7/41
Russell, J. B., M.C. (Lt. late M.G. Corps.)	21/ 7/41
Eakins, G. W., M.C. (Capt. late R. Scots.)	21/ 7/41

Adjutant & Quarter-Master
Duncan, Capt. (actg. 16/5/41)
C. G., Gen. List Inf.　　　16/ 5/41

2nd Lieutenants

Adams, T. A.	1/ 2/41
Bruce, J., M.M.	1/ 2/41
Cramond, J. I.	1/ 2/41
Cunningham, J., M.M.	1/ 2/41
Dunford, C. R.	1/ 2/41
Dyer, C. T.	1/ 2/41
Jones, J. V.	1/ 2/41
Macdonald, A.	1/ 2/41
Mackenzie, T. J., (Lt. late A. & S.H.)	1/ 2/41
Newton, H.	1/ 2/41
Robinson, A. B.	1/ 2/41
Wright, L. G.	1/ 2/41
Balfour, R. L.	1/ 2/41
Wood, J.	1/ 2/41
Robertson, J. T.	20/ 6/41
Richards, J. C. D.	21/ 7/41
Borland, J.	21/ 7/41
Livingston, J. A.	21/ 7/41
Sharples, H.	21/ 7/41

Medical Officer

6th CITY OF EDINBURGH BATTALION

Lt.-Colonel
Walker, J.   1/ 2/41

Majors
Inglis, J. M.   1/ 2/41
Aitken, A. C., T.D., (Maj.
  late R. Scots.)   1/ 2/41
Buchan, D. C., (2/Lt. late
  R.A.F.)   1/ 2/41
Mure, A. H., T.D., (Col. late
  T.A.)   1/ 2/41
Wilson, G., M.C., (Capt. late
  R.T.R.)   1/ 2/41
Munro, D.   1/ 2/41
Black, J. B., (Maj. late
  Camerons)   1/ 2/41
Anderson, J.   26/ 6/41
Glen, A., M.C., (Maj. late
  Black Watch)   26/ 6/41
Fraser, J. H. (Lt. late
  Black Watch)   30/ 7/41

Captains
Alexander, J. A., (Capt. late
  K.O.S.B.)   1/ 2/41
Caskey, R. W.   1/ 2/41
Clark, A. T.   1/ 2/41
Gordon, J.   1/ 2/41
Inglis, T. H.   1/ 2/41
Loundon, J. W.   1/ 2/41
Mitchell, J.   1/ 2/41
56455-3(53)

Captains - contd.
Powney, C. C.   1/ 2/41
Maitland, J. (Capt. late
  D.L.I.)   14/ 5/41
Tough, R. M.   7/ 6/41
Fraser, H. B.   26/ 6/41
Gray, T.   26/ 6/41
Dandie, A. S. O., (Lt.
  late R.G.A.)   30/ 6/41
Watson, W. D. (2/Lt. late
  Black Watch)   26/ 7/41

Lieutenants
Cloughley, D. T.   1/ 2/41
Coull, J. B. W.   1/ 2/41
Duncan, W. B.   1/ 2/41
Evans, T.   1/ 2/41
Ferguson, J. McK.   1/ 2/41
Franklin, T. H.   1/ 2/41
Gray, P. B.   1/ 2/41
Gordon, A. T., (Lt. late
  M.G. Corps)   1/ 2/41
Jeffrey, F. J.   1/ 2/41
Johnston, J., (Capt. late
  Gordons)   1/ 2/41
Kidd, G. A.   1/ 2/41
Laird, W. A.   1/ 2/41
Makin, A.   1/ 2/41
Matheson, R. P., M.C.,
  (Capt. late Can. Mil. Forces) 1/ 2/41
Morrison, A. B.   1/ 2/41
Pringle-Pattison, N. S.,
  (Capt. late R. Scots.)   1/ 2/41
Rands, E. G.   1/ 2/41
Ross, J.   1/ 2/41
Rutty, E. C., M.M.   1/ 2/41
Shearer, G. (Lt. late The
  King's R.)   1/ 2/41
Stewart, P., M.C., (Capt.
  late H.L.I.)   1/ 2/41

EDINBURGH AREA - contd.

CITY OF EDINBURGH ZONE - contd.

6th City of Edinburgh Battalion - contd.

Lieutenants - contd.		2nd Lieutenants - contd.	
Turner, J., O.B.E., M.C.,		Patch, C. M.	1/ 2/41
(Capt. late Can. Mil. Forces)	1/ 2/41	Rendall, W. C.	1/ 2/41
Watson, N.	1/ 2/41	Smail, J. B.	1/ 2/41
Watt, A. D.	1/ 2/41	Stevenson, D.	1/ 2/41
Anderson, G. A. (Capt. late		Valentine, I. A. H.	1/ 2/41
K.O.S.B.)	1/ 2/41	Welsh, W. A., (Capt. late	
Wright, W. MacK.	1/ 2/41	Border R.)	1/ 2/41
Brunt, G. W. G.	1/ 2/41	Williams, S. H.	1/ 2/41
Blackwood, P. P.	1/ 6/41	Inglis, G.	1/ 2/41
Kinnear, A. McG.	1/ 6/41	Cairns, W. T. H.	1/ 2/41
Shiels, J. B., M.C., D.C.M.,		Elliot, B. A.	1/ 2/41
M.M.	26/ 6/41	Perkin, W. F. M.	1/ 2/41
Ireland, M. J. N. (2/Lt. late		Thomson, J. B.	25/ 6/41
R.A.F.)	26/ 6/41	Wallace, R. B., (Lt. late	
Spark, A. D., (Maj. Res.		R. Scots.)	26/ 6/41
of Off.)	26/ 6/41	Imrie, R. S.	26/ 6/41
Munro, A. S. M.	26/ 6/41	Muir, R.	24/ 7/41
Macdonald, J. G. (Lt. late		Adams, R.	25/ 7/41
R. Scots)	26/ 6/41		
Palmer, B.	26/ 6/41		
Robertson, J. H. C.	24/ 7/41		
Curran, J., M.M.	24/ 7/41		
Stout, J.	24/ 7/41		
Foley, J. E.	24/ 7/41		
Mitchell, J. G.	25/ 7/41		
Jackson, S. E.	7/ 8/41	Adjutant & Quarter-Master	
Bracken, A.	7/ 8/41		

2nd Lieutenants			
Benzies, W.	1/ 2/41		
Boswell, J.	1/ 2/41	Medical Officers	
Drysdale, C. S.	1/ 2/41	Millar, Maj. A. F. W., (Lt.	
Falconer, P. A., (2/Lt.		late R.A.M.C.)	1/ 2/41
late R.G.A.)	1/ 2/41	Ronaldson, Capt. R. M.,	
Grieve, J. G.	1/ 2/41	M.D., F.R.C.P.	14/ 7/41
Hall, A. D.	1/ 2/41		
Hampton, R. O.	1/ 2/41		
Jefferson, W. E.	1/ 2/41		
Kellock, D. G.	1/ 2/41		
Marshall, R.	1/ 2/41		
Morrison, W.	1/ 2/41		
Macadum, J.	1/ 2/41		

EDINBURGH AREA - contd.

CITY OF EDINBURGH ZONE - contd.

7th CITY OF EDINBURGH (MUSSELBURGH)
BATTALION

Lt.-Colonel

Amour, J., M.C., (Capt.
late T.A.)   1/ 2/41

Majors

Osborne, J., (Lt. late
A. & S.H.)   1/ 2/41
Aitken, G.   1/ 2/41
Corbett, G. F.   1/ 2/41
Greenlees, J. R. C., D.S.O.,
(Lt.-Col. late R.A.M.C.)   1/ 2/41
Maxwell, G.   1/ 2/41
Thomson, T., (Lt. late
R. Scots)   1/ 2/41
Mavor, A. B.   26/ 7/41

Captains

Clark, G. H.   1/ 2/41
Lowe, A. G. R.   1/ 2/41
Morpard, A. T., (Capt. Gen.
List. T.A.)   1/ 2/41
Murray, A.   1/ 2/41
Riddell, A.   1/ 2/41
Wilson, D. M.   1/ 2/41
Wood, D. H.   1/ 2/41
Stiven, D. S., M.C., (Lt.
late R. Scots.)   1/ 7/41
Edwards, G. F., M.M.   26/ 7/41

Lieutenants

Babb, H. C.   1/ 2/41
Brash, A. B.   1/ 2/41
Clarkson, G. H.   1/ 2/41
Collyns, C. H. A., (2/Lt. late
R.F.C.)   1/ 2/41
Currie, H.   1/ 2/41
Davidson, W.   1/ 2/41
Goodacre, R.   1/ 2/41
Halliday, D.   1/ 2/41
Maclagan-Wedderburn, A. S.   1/ 2/41

Lieutenants - contd.

McLaren, J.   1/ 2/41
McPherson, T.   1/ 2/41
Mitchell, J.   1/ 2/41
Musson, W. A. J.   1/ 2/41
Snell, B. C.   1/ 2/41
Stagg, J.   1/ 2/41
Stewart, A. G.   1/ 2/41
Storie, J.   1/ 2/41
Turnbull, A.   1/ 2/41
Wilson, G. L.   1/ 2/41
Potts, W. G.   26/ 7/41

2nd Lieutenants

Bolton, D.   1/ 2/41
Brown, A. K.   1/ 2/41
Cleland, J., M.M.   1/ 2/41
Gordon, A.   1/ 2/41
McDonald, A.   1/ 2/41
Moffat, A.   1/ 2/41
Rankin, A. C. D.   1/ 2/41
Russell, W.   1/ 2/41
Shiel, T. C.   1/ 2/41
Smith, A.   1/ 2/41
Shenhouse, J. A.   1/ 2/41
Wallace, R. H. H.   11/ 2/41
Wood, A. S.   15/ 7/41

Adjutant & Quarter-Master

Medical Officer

Laing, Maj., F. C.   1/ 2/41

EDINBURGH AREA - contd.

CITY OF EDINBURGH ZONE - contd.

8th CITY OF EDINBURGH BATTALION

Lt.-Colonel
Robertson, K. S., O.B.E., (Maj.
late R. Scots)   1/ 2/41

Majors
Pringle, J. D., (Capt. late
R. Scots)   1/ 2/41
Macdonald, J., (Capt. late
K.A. Rif.)   1/ 2/41.
McDavid, J. (Capt. late
R.S. Fus.)   1/ 2/41
Grahame, T., T.D., (Lt.-Col.
late T.A. Res.)   1/ 2/41
Cooper, W. R., (Maj. late
R. Scots.)   1/ 2/41
Nisbet, W. H.   1/ 2/41
Ramsden, H. S., (Capt. late
R.A.S.C.)   1/ 2/41

Captains
Stoddart, A. K., (2/Lt. late
R. Scots.)   1/ 2/41
Little, A. C. W., M.C., (Lt.
late R.A.)   1/ 2/41
Cochrane, J. D.   1/ 2/41
Langdon, R. T., (F/O. late
R.A.F.)   1/ 2/41
Johnson, R., D.C.M.   1/ 6/41
Fiskin, A. J.   20/ 6/41

Lieutenants
Ted, D.   1/ 2/41
Macfarlane, P. R. C.   1/ 2/41
Smith, R.   1/ 2/41
Usher, T., (F/O late R.A.F.)   1/ 2/41
Mullens, E. W., (Capt. Gen.
List T.A.)   1/ 2/41
Dickson, W., (Capt. Gen.
List. T.A.)   1/ 2/41
Wainwright, M. L., M.M.   1/ 2/41
Morgan, D. O.   1/ 2/41
McLarty, M. R.   1/ 2/41

Lieutenants - contd.
Wood, R. I.   1/ 2/41
Campbell, J. D.   1/ 2/41
Ritchie, T. D. (Lt. late
Black Watch)   1/ 2/41
Dunn, J. (Capt. late K.O.S.B.)   1/ 2/41
Smith, J. R. F., (Capt.
late R.F.A.)   1/ 2/41
Peapell, H. N.   1/ 2/41
Sleigh, W. L., (2/Lt. late
R.A.S.C.)   1/ 2/41
Harkess, G. L.   1/ 6/41
McIvor, A.   20/ 6/41

2nd Lieutenants
Aitken, R. C.   1/ 2/41
Sinclair, I. S. R.   1/ 2/41
Crawford, W. B. A.   1/ 2/41
Sutherland, G. R.   1/ 2/41
Smith, J. R. M.   1/ 2/41
Butt, G.   1/ 2/41
Anderson, J. L.   1/ 2/41
Hall-Patch, P. K. J.   1/ 2/41
Campbell, J. G.   1/ 2/41
Pook, H. L.   1/ 2/41
McCombie, H. W. T.   1/ 2/41
Thomson, L. S.   1/ 2/41
Waterman, F. W., M.C.,
(Capt. late Can. Mil. Forces)   1/ 2/41
Heron, A. B.   1/ 2/41
Taylor, A. Mc. I.   20/ 6/41

Adjutant & Quarter-Master

Medical Officer
Haultain, Maj., W. F. T., O.B.E.,
M.C., F.R.C.S., M.R.C.P.,
(Maj. late R.A.M.C.)   1/ 2/41

10th CITY OF EDINBURGH (3rd L.N.E.R.)
BATTALION

Lt.-Colonel
Trask, E. D., (late R.A.F.)   1/ 2/41

Majors
Ings, W. E. C., (Capt. late
R. Fus.)   1/ 2/41
Matthewson-Dick, T.   1/ 2/41
Dunlop, J. B.   1/ 2/41
Lund, G. H. K.   1/ 2/41
McLeod, N., (Capt. late
Inniskilling Fus.)   1/ 2/41
Mein, A. B., (2/Lt. late
R. Scots)   1/ 2/41

Captains
Lisle, J., M.M.   1/ 2/41
Philip, W. T.   1/ 2/41
Tweeddale, G.   1/ 2/41
McLeod, W. J.   14/ 5/41
Gray, W. B.   2/ 8/41

Lieutenants
Anderson, C. E. S.   1/ 2/41
Arthur, J. A., (2/Lt. late
R. Scots)   1/ 2/41
Broomfield, R. H.   1/ 2/41
Cameron, A.   1/ 2/41
Campbell, N.   1/ 2/41
Cox, J. R.   1/ 2/41
Dunn, D. A.   1/ 2/41
Ferguson, D.   1/ 2/41
Manson, E. M.   1/ 2/41
McLeish, D.   1/ 2/41
Paterson, G. (Capt. late
R.E.)   1/ 2/41

Lieutenants – contd.
Robertson, J.   1/ 2/41
Strachan, J.   1/ 2/41
Ogston, J.   1/ 6/41
Davies, G. P.   1/ 6/41
Stupart, D.   1/ 6/41
Brannan, W.   25/ 7/41
McIntosh, J.   25/ 7/41

2nd Lieutenants
Armstrong, A. S.   1/ 2/41
Brown, A.   1/ 2/41
Goodfellow, J.   1/ 2/41
Hossack, G. J.   1/ 2/41
Elliot, J. W.   1/ 2/41
Laurie, T. A.   1/ 2/41
Rankine, C.   1/ 2/41
Hair, T. A.   12/ 6/41
Yorke, T. E.   16/ 6/41
Fairgrieve, B. N., D.C.M.   25/ 7/41
Linkston, C.   25/ 7/41

Adjutant & Quarter-Master
Ross, Capt. (actg. 23/4/41)
D., Gen. List Inf.   23/ 4/41

Medical Officer

11th CITY OF EDINBURGH (11th G.P.O.)
         BATTALION

Lt.-Colonel
Cameron, A., (Lt. late T.A.)   1/ 2/41

Majors
Atkinson, J.   1/ 2/41
Brunton, J. B.   1/ 2/41
Howard, J. L.   1/ 2/41
Moncrieff, A. Y., (Lt. late
   R.A.F.)   1/ 2/41
Murray, J.   1/ 2/41
Todd, H., M.C., M.M., (Capt.
   late A. & S.H.)   1/ 2/41

Captains
Cruickshank, A. L.   1/ 2/41
Skea, J.   1/ 2/41
Watson, T. W.   1/ 2/41

Lieutenants
Gleed, A. A.   1/ 2/41
Arthur, C. S.   1/ 2/41
Balgarnie, J.   1/ 2/41
Borland, J.   1/ 2/41
Burns, R.   1/ 2/41
Clephane, H., M.M. (2/Lt. late
   R. Scots)   1/ 2/41
Gregor, F. C. L., M.M.   1/ 2/41
Liddle, J.   1/ 2/41
Marjoribanks, T.   1/ 2/41
Mackay, P. W., (Capt. late
   Black Watch)   1/ 2/41
McWalter, W. V.   1/ 2/41
Ross, J. B. S.   1/ 2/41
Ross, W.   1/ 2/41
Stephenson, W. L.   1/ 2/41
Smith, R.   1/ 2/41

2nd Lieutenants
England, A. G.   1/ 2/41
Hannan, A.   1/ 2/41
Hay, N.   1/ 2/41
Maguire, J.   1/ 2/41
McIvor, D.   1/ 2/41
Rankin, J. G., M.C.   1/ 2/41

Adjutant & Quarter-Master
Brown, Capt. (actg. 25/4/41)
   I., Gen. List Inf.   25/ 4/41

Medical Officer

EDINBURGH AREA SIGNALS COMPANY

Major
Carswell, J. I. (Lt. late R.E.) 1/ 2/41

Captain
Buchanan, H. B. (Lt. late
   R.A.S.C.)   1/ 2/41

Lieutenant
Smith, W. C. B.   1/ 2/41

EDINBURGH AREA - contd.

LOTHIAN ZONE

Commander	Blair, Col. P. J., D.S.O., T.D., (Col. T.A.) 1/ 2/41
Assistant to Commander	McIntyre, Maj. J. G., M.C. (Capt. late R.S. Fus.) 1/ 2/41
Assistant Signal Officer	Dickson, Lt., W. F. (Capt. late R. Ir. Fus.) 1/ 2/41
Liaison Officer	Ramsay, Capt. Sir James D., Bt., M.V.O., T.D., (Lt.-Col. late T.A.) 1/ 8/41
Weapon Training Officer	Robertson, Capt. C., (Lt. late R.A.M.C.) 1/ 2/41
Staff Officers	Bennet-Clark, Capt., T. W. (Lt.-Col. T.A. Res.) Anderson, Capt. H. L. 1/ 2/41
Intelligence Officer	Ogilvie, Capt., A. G., O.B.E., (Capt. late R.F.A.) 1/ 2/41
Signal Officer	Walkden, Capt. J. S. 1/ 2/41

Territorial Army Association administering	City of Edinburgh T.A. Association, 19, Palmerston Place, Edinburgh.

1st MIDLOTHIAN BATTALION

Lt.-Colonel
Paul, J. W. B., D.S.O., V.D., (Col. late Ceylon Mtd. Rif.) 1/ 2/41

Majors
Barnet, W., (2/Lt. late R. Scots) 1/ 2/41
Birrell, E. T. F., C.B., C.M.G., (Col. late R.A.M.C.) 1/ 2/41
Dundas, Sir Philip, Bt., (Lt. late Lothian & Border Horse) 1/ 2/41
Eddison, J. H., M.C., (Maj. late R.F.A.) 1/ 2/41
Ferguson, D. M. 1/ 2/41
Thomson, J. F. G., (Lt. late R. Scots) 1/ 2/41
Prenter, R. G., (Lt. late R.N.) 1/ 2/41
Ramsay, D. M., (Lt. late R.A.S.C) 1/ 2/41
Urquhart, W. M., (Maj. late R. Scots) 1/ 2/41
Watherston, R. H. 1/ 2/41
Stuart, W., D.S.O., (Maj. late T.A. 1/ 2/41

Captains
Kay, J. C. 1/ 2/41
McNeill, D., (Lt. late R.G.A.) 1/ 2/41

Captains - contd.
Moodie, D., (Lt. late M.G. Corps) 1/ 2/41
Philips, R. C., (Lt. late R.S. Fus.) 1/ 2/41
Preston, J., D.S.O., (Lt. late Cameronians) 1/ 2/41
Pringle, J. 1/ 2/41
Sharp, H. G., (Capt. late R.F.A.) 1/ 2/41
Stirling, J., (Capt. late T.A. Res.) 1/ 2/41
McKinnon, J. W., M.C., (Maj. Res. of Off.) 1/ 2/41

Lieutenants
Baird, B. 1/ 2/41
Bourhill, P., (Lt. late R. Scots) 1/ 2/41
Campbell, A. N. C. 1/ 2/41
Chatfield, A. W. F., (2/Lt. late The Queen's R.) 1/ 2/41
Dodds, F. D. 1/ 2/41
Eckford, W. R. 1/ 2/41
Elliot, T., (2/Lt. late R.A.S.C.) 1/ 2/41

82

1st MIDLOTHIAN BATTALION - contd.

Lieutenants - contd.			2nd Lieutenants	
Elliot, W. I. (2/Lt. late			Anderson, J.	1/ 2/41
Border R.)	1/ 2/41		Anderson, R.	1/ 2/41
Elton, R. R.	1/ 2/41		Bruce, J.	1/ 2/41
Fisher, A. C.	1/ 2/41		Calwell, W. N.	1/ 2/41
Glenney, J.	1/ 2/41		Cobban, J.	1/ 2/41
Gray, J.	1/ 2/41		Davie, J. A.	1/ 2/41
Gray, W. H.	1/ 2/41		Dugan, H.	1/ 2/41
Hamilton, W. H.	1/ 2/41		Elliott, R., (2/Lt. late	
Harper, J., M.C., (Lt. late			M.G. Corps)	1/ 2/41
R.E.)	1/ 2/41		Esson, W.	1/ 2/41
Harwell, J. H.	1/ 2/41		Fairgrieve, T.	1/ 2/41
Hastie, A.	1/ 2/41		Fairgrieve, T. D.	1/ 2/41
Herdman, J.	1/ 2/41		Forrest, J.	1/ 2/41
Hogg, R. N., (Lt. late T.A.)	1/ 2/41		Frew, D.	1/ 2/41
Ingram, C. W., (Maj. late R.E.)	1/ 2/41		Garrett, A. S.	1/ 2/41
Kerr, A. P. B., (2/Lt. late			Greenock, A. D.	1/ 2/41
T.A.)	1/ 2/41		Grieve, A. S., M.C.	1/ 2/41
Kerr, S. K. G.	1/ 2/41		Handley, J. S.	1/ 2/41
Kerr, J., (2/Lt. late T.A.)	1/ 2/41		Hastie, T.	1/ 2/41
Laurie, R.	1/ 2/41		Hole, G. L. D., (Lt. late	
McIntyre, R. W. M.	1/ 8/41		T.A.)	1/ 2/41
Mann, J. C. W.	1/ 2/41		Loughran, J. D.	1/ 2/41
Poustie, J. T., (Lt. late			MacEwan, N.	1/ 2/41
K.O.S.B.)	1/ 2/41		Murphy, S.	1/ 2/41
Douglas, A., (Lt. late			Murray, R.	1/ 2/41
R. Scots)	1/ 2/41		Paterson, D.	1/ 2/41
Shearer, W., (Capt. late			Syme, S. B.	1/ 2/41
R.A.F.)	1/ 2/41		Wilson, A.	1/ 2/41
Russell, R. S.	1/ 2/41		Davie, J. (Capt. late R.F.A.)	1/ 2/41
Russell, W.	1/ 2/41		Linton, J. M.M.	30/ 6/41
Saffery, P. W.	1/ 2/41		Kerr, J.	1/ 7/41
Somerville, H. C., (Maj. late			Deenan, P.	10/ 7/41
Worc. R.)	1/ 2/41		Brown, R.	1/ 8/41
Telfer, W., M.M.	1/ 2/41		Oswald, J., O.B.E. (Capt. late	
Tod, A. K., (Capt. late			R.E.)	1/ 8/41
R. Scots)	1/ 2/41			
Wallace, J.	1/ 2/41		Adjutant & Quarter-Master	
Watt, J.	1/ 2/41		Donaldson, Capt. actg.	
Vaugh, J.	1/ 2/41		20/3/41) R. M., R. Scots.	20/ 3/41
Wilson, A. S. B.	1/ 2/41			
Finlay, A.	1/ 2/41		Medical Officer	
Kohler, F. E., (2/Lt. late			Gray, Maj., G. D., C.B.E.	
R.A.)	1/ 2/41		(Lt.-Col. late R.A.M.C.)	1/ 2/41
Bonar, J. J., (Capt. late				
R.T.R.)	1/ 6/41			
Kay, R. (Capt. late H.L.I.)	23/ 6/41			

1st EAST LOTHIAN BATTALION

Lt.-Colonel
O'Brien, Hon. H. B., M.C.,
(Capt. late I. Gds.)   1/ 2/41

Majors
Barr, A. G., O.B.E., (Lt./Pmr.
late R.A.P.C.)   1/ 2/41
Blake, D. J., M.C., (Lt. late
R.F.A.)   1/ 2/41
Gibson, F. P.   1/ 2/41
Gillespie, G. M., M.C.,
(Capt. late Seaforth)   1/ 2/41
Mather, R. M., (Capt. late
R.E.)   1/ 2/41
Ross, J. D., (Lt. late
R. Scots.)   1/ 2/41
Tweeddale, The Marq. of,
(Maj. late F.F.A.)   1/ 2/41
Strachan, J. C. (Lt.-Col.
late R.A.)   1/ 2/41
Watson, T. W. (Capt. late
R. Scots.)   1/ 2/41

Captains
Bell, J.   .   1/ 2/41
Burns, A.   1/ 2/41
Durham, J. A. R., O.B.E.,
(Capt. late Gordons)   1/ 2/41
Paterson, H., (2/Lt. late
R. Scots.)   1/ 2/41
Stevenson, A. C., (2/Lt. late
R.A.S.C.)   1/ 2/41
Slight, M. A.   1/ 2/41
Beveridge, H. V.   1/ 2/41
St. John, E. F., C.M.G., D.S.O.,
(Col. ret. pay)   16/ 7/41

Lieutenants
Broomfield, D., (2/Lt.
late K.O.S.B.)   1/ 2/41
Brown, J.   1/ 2/41
Clark, J. G. D.   1/ 2/41
Dale, J. R.   1/ 2/41
Darling, D.   1/ 2/41
Hamilton-Dalrymple, Sir
Hew C. Bt.   1/ 2/41
Davidson, J.   1/ 2/41
Dower, H., (2/Lt. late
R. Scots)   1/ 2/41
Durham, A. W. R.   1/ 2/41
Fraser, G., M.C., (Capt. late
A. & S.H.)   1/ 2/41
Gibson, G. P.   1/ 2/41
Henderson, I. C.   1/ 2/41
Inglis, A.   1/ 2/41
Lees, D. S. C.   1/ 2/41
Logan, J.   1/ 2/41
Mackintosh, H. J.   1/ 2/41

Lieutenants - contd.
McLennan, A. J. R.   1/ 2/41
Malcolm, T. A.   1/ 2/41
Moffat, J. B., M.M.   1/ 2/41
Morrison, W. C.   1/ 2/41
Patrick, R., (Capt. late
R.F.A.)   1/ 2/41
Prentice, P. F., (Lt. late
Camerons)   1/ 2/41
Rattray, J.   1/ 2/41
Russell, W. N.   1/ 2/41
Shepherd, T.   1/ 2/41
Simpson, L. S., C.B.E., D.S.O.
(Col. late R.E.)   1/ 2/41
Smith, J. J. E.   1/ 2/41
Tweedie, A. J. (2/Lt. late
R. Scots.)   1/ 2/41
Wallace, H. O.   1/ 2/41
Watson, R. G.   1/ 2/41
Watt, W. O., (F/O. late
R.A.F.)   1/ 2/41
Wilkie, D. D.   1/ 2/41
Henderson, J. M.   1/ 2/41
Purves, A. M.   1/ 2/41
Taylor, J.   1/ 2/41
Tapt, J.   20/ 6/41
Fraser, G.   21/ 6/41
Watt, W. R.   27/ 6/41

2nd Lieutenants
Blair, A.   1/ 2/41
Brotherston, A.   1/ 2/41
Buchanan, G. E. C.   1/ 2/41
Cadzow, D. J., (2/Lt. late R.A.)1/ 2/41
Dodds, J. J. G.   1/ 2/41
Durie, F.   1/ 2/41
Forbes, J. L.   1/ 2/41
Fortune, J.   1/ 2/41
Gibson, G. A.   1/ 2/41
Hannah, G. A.   1/ 2/41
Miller, H. W.   1/ 2/41
Reid, A.   1/ 2/41
Robertson, J. G.   1/ 2/41
Smith, G. F., (Lt. late R.Scots.)   1/ 2/41
Walls, G. L. M.   1/ 2/41
Thomson, A. M. B.   1/ 2/41
Forrest, A. S.   1/ 2/41
Robson, J.   6/ 6/41
Rintoul, R., D.C.M.   12/ 6/41
Kennedy, A.   3/ 7/41
Young, D. C.   17/ 7/41
Cunninghame, G. Y.   17/ 7/41

Adjutant & Quarter-Master

Medical Officer
Strachan, Maj., J. C.
(Capt. late T.A. Res.)   1/ 2/41

84

1st WEST LOTHIAN BATTALION

Lt.-Colonel
Hope, The Lord, (Maj. late T.A.) — 1/ 2/41

Majors
Clarkson, H. K. (Capt. late R.F.A.) — 1/ 2/41
Aitken, D., (Lt. late R. Scots) — 1/ 2/41
Brebner, R. F., (Maj. late
 Cameronians) — 1/ 2/41
Lyall, J. — 1/ 2/41
Morton, J., (F/O. late R.A.F.) — 1/ 2/41
Robson, W. G. — 1/ 2/41
Shaw, J. N., M.C., (Capt. late
 R.Scots) — 1/ 2/41
Stothard, G. M. — 1/ 2/41
Walker, T. J., (Lt. late R.F.A.) — 1/ 2/41
Warren, D. B., O.B.E., (Maj. late
 H.L.I.) — 1/ 2/41
Henderson, W. A., M.C., (Lt. late
 R.Scots) — 1/ 2/41

Captains
Arrol, C., (Lt. late R.A.S.C.) — 1/ 2/41
Brydon, T., (Capt. late R.Scots) — 1/ 2/41
Clancy, M. J. — 1/ 2/41
Dewar, J. T. — 1/ 2/41
Kerr, A. — 1/ 2/41
McIntosh, J., D.C.M. — 1/ 2/41
Rutherford, C. N., (Lt. late
 H.L.I.) — 1/ 2/41
Smith, G. H., M.C., (2/Lt. late
 R.T.R.) — 1/ 2/41
Smillie, H. — 1/ 2/41
Steele, J. — 1/ 2/41
Walker, F. H. N. — 1/ 7/41
Robertson, A. F. (2/Lt. late
 R.Scots) — 21/ 7/41

Lieutenants
Allison, D. — 1/ 2/41
Black, C. — 1/ 2/41
Blackwood, P. H. G. — 1/ 2/41
Boyd, A. — 1/ 2/41
Brash, F. — 1/ 2/41
Caldwell, J. M., (2/Lt. late
 R.A.F.) — 1/ 2/41
Carlaw, J. — 1/ 2/41
Carstairs, J. — 1/ 2/41
Close, T., M.M. — 1/ 2/41
Cowell, G. T. — 1/ 2/41
Dickson, R. A. — 1/ 2/41
Drylie, J. E. — 1/ 2/41
Fleming, E. — 1/ 2/41
Groat, J., M.M. — 1/ 2/41
Hannah, W. — 1/ 2/41
Wheatley, R. J., M.C., (Lt. late
 M.G. Corps.) — 1/ 2/41
Johnston, J. — 1/ 2/41
Loch, D. — 1/ 2/41

Lieu   contd.
Miller, W. — 1/ 2/4
McArthur, J. B. — 1/ 2/4
McGowan, H. — 1/ 2/4
McIvor, A. — 1/ 2/4
Macknight, G. S. — 1/ 2/4
Miller, R., (2/Lt. late
 Camerons) — 1/ 2/4
Moffat, A. — 1/ 2/4
Morrison, A. R. — 1/ 2/4
Nicol, T. — 1/ 2/4
Provan, J. — 1/ 2/4
Pyper, G. H. — 1/ 2/4
Russell, J. — 1/ 2/4
Scott, W. G. F. — 1/ 2/4
Sinclair, R. T. K. — 1/ 2/4
Stevenson, W. Y. — 1/ 2/4
Stirling, W. M. — 1/ 2/4
Tennant, D. D. S. — 1/ 2/4
Thomson, W. N. — 1/ 2/41
Walker, A. — 1/ 2/4
Whiteford, R. — 1/ 2/41
Wilson, R. — 1/ 2/41
Scott, W. W. — 1/ 2/41
Duncan, W. — 1/ 2/41
Millar, W. — 1/ 2/41
Scott, J. — 1/ 2/41
Young, A. T., (2/Lt. late
 R.A.F.) — 1/ 2/41
Sharp, W. S. — 1/ 6/41
Jeffrey, A. W. — 12/ 7/41
Anderson, S. — 21/ 7/41

2nd Lieutenants
Boyd, D. — 1/ 2/41
Burns, W., M.C., (Maj. late
 M.G. Corps) — 1/ 2/41
Cochrane, D. A. — 1/ 2/41
Dudgeon, A. N. — 1/ 2/41
Fleming, T. H. — 1/ 2/41
Forrest, J. S. C. — 1/ 2/41
Gordon, J. A. A. D. W. — 1/ 2/41
MacCullum, G., M.M. — 1/ 2/41
Murdoch, G. — 1/ 2/41
Paxton, A. — 1/ 2/41
Ritchie, J. M. — 1/ 2/41
Robertson, J. R. — 1/ 2/41
Ross, A. — 1/ 2/41
Stewart-Clark, A. — 1/ 2/41
Struth, W. — 1/ 2/41
Wright, J. — 1/ 2/41
Wood, J. — 1/ 2/41

1st West Lothian Battalion - contd.

2nd Lieutenants - contd.

Simpson, H. F.	1/ 2/41
Brown, A. G.	1/ 2/41
Herd, W.	1/ 2/41
Longmuir, V. S.	1/ 2/41
Gray, J.	1/ 2/41
Edwards, J.	1/ 2/41
Aikman, J. McA.	25/ 6/41
Broome, W. W.	25/ 6/41
Clunie, F. G.	25/ 8/41
Cunningham, A.	25/ 6/41
McMillan, H.	25/ 6/41
Nimmo, J. W.	25/ 6/41
Sinclair, P. W.	25/ 6/41
Walker, R.	25/ 6/41
White, A. B.	25/ 6/41
Clelland, D. R.	25/ 6/41
Lowe, D.	21/ 7/41
Crichton, R.	21/ 7/41
Baxter, J.	28/ 7/41

Adjutant & Quarter-Master

Medical Officers

Anderson, Maj. W., O.B.E., M.B., (Maj. late R.A.M.C.)	1/ 2/41
Orr, Capt. J. F.	21/ 7/41
Graham, Capt. J. S., M.B.	21/ 7/41
Shafto, Capt. W. A., M.D. (Maj. late R.A.M.C.)	21/ 7/41

1st PEEBLESSHIRE BATTALION

.Lt.-Colonel

Thorburn, W., D.S.O. (Lt.-Col. ret. T.A.)	1/ 2/41

Majors

Sutherland, A. H. C., O.B.E., M.C., (Lt.-Col. late Black Watch)	1/ 2/41
Thomson, E. G., M.C., (Maj. late R.G.A.)	1/ 2/41
Thorburn, R. M., (Capt. late T.A.)	1/ 2/41
Thorburn, W. H., (Maj. late T.A.)	1/ 2/41
Gair, D.	1/ 2/41

Captains

Nicolson, J. G. G., (Lt. late H.L.I.)	1/ 2/41
Kennedy, L. A., M.C., (Capt. late Can. Mil. Forces)	1/ 2/41
Mitchell, H. N., (2/Lt. K.O.S.B.)	1/ 2/41
Macdonald, R. J., (Lt. late K.O.S.B.)	14/ 6/41

Lieutenants

Brown, C. M., (Capt. late Gordons)	1/ 2/41
Robb, G. D. (Capt. late Gordons)	1/ 2/41
Johnston, W.	1/ 2/41
Ballantyne, T. D.	1/ 2/41
Euman, J. R., (Lt. late H.L.I.)	1/ 2/41
Dundas, J. D., (2/Lt. late R. Scots.)	1/ 2/41
Hay, Sir Duncan E., Bt., (Lt. late Gen. List)	1/ 2/41
Scarth, A. D., (2/Lt. late Gordons)	1/ 2/41
Elwell, B. L., (Lt. late K.O.S.B.)	1/ 2/41
Hamilton, A.	1/ 2/41
Thorburn, M. P., (Capt. late R. Scots.)	1/ 2/41
Balfour, F. R. S.	1/ 2/41
Thomson, R. J., (Capt. late Border R.)	1/ 2/41
Dyer, E. (Capt. late Seaforth)	1/ 2/41

2nd Lieutenants

Williamson, R. L.	1/ 2/41
Jardine, J.	1/ 2/41
Reid, W. C., (2/Lt. late R.E.)	1/ 2/41
Taylor, G. S.	1/ 2/41
Ballantyne, H., (Lt. late R.N.V.R.)	1/ 2/41
Waldie, J.	1/ 2/41
Miller-Thomas, W. C., (Lt. late R. Scots.)	1/ 2/41
Richard, A. M., (Capt. late R. Scots.)	1/ 2/41
Smart, J.	1/ 2/41
Anderson, D.	1/ 2/41
Dickson, H. E.	1/ 2/41

Adjutant & Quarter-Master

Thorburn, Capt. (actg. 28/4/41) R. M., R. Scots.	28/ 4/41

Medical Officers

Bryce, Maj., W. H., M.B., (Maj. late R.A.M.C.)	1/ 2/41
Bowie, Capt. J. D., D.S.O.	1/ 2/41
Graham-Yooll, Capt., R. W., M.B.	1/ 7/41

EDINBURGH AREA - contd.

SCOTTISH BORDER ZONE

Commander	Contstable-Maxwell-Scott, Col., Sir Walter J., Bt., C.B., .S.O., (Maj.- Gen. ret. pay) (Res. of Off.) 1/ 2/41
Second-in-Command	Montgomery, Lt.-Col. B., (Capt. late T.A.) 1/ 2/41
Assistant to Commander	Agnew, Maj., H. C., O.B.E. (Col. late R.E.) 1/ 2/41
Staff Officer	Ewing, Capt., I. A. (Maj. late T.A.) 1/ 2/41
Liaison Officer	Greig, Capt. J. 1/ 2/41
P.A.D. & Gas Officer	Home, Capt. R. G. (Capt. late Black Watch) 26/ 6/41
Chief Guide	Hepburne-Scott, Capt., Hon. W. S. (Capt. late T.A.) 4/ 7/41
Territorial Army Association administering	Roxburgh, Berwick & Selkirk T.A. Association, Glen Douglas, Jedburgh.

1st SCOTTISH BORDER BATTALION
Lt.-Colonel

Majors

Laing, P. L. P., T.D., (Maj. late K.O.S.B.)	1/ 2/41
Aitken, A., (Lt. late S. Stafford R.)	1/ 2/41
Brown, P. G., C.B.E., (Capt. R.N.)	1/ 2/41
Dodd, J. J., (Lt. late Ind. Army)	1/ 2/41
Merchant, S.	1/ 2/41
Secon, J. P., (Lt. ret.)	1/ 2/41
Usher, H., M.C., (Capt. late M.G. Corps)	8/ 5/41
Renwick, J. A. P., M.C., (Lt. late K.O.S.B.)	22/ 6/41

Captains

Inglis, J. M.	1/ 2/41
McGivern, A. W.	1/ 2/41
Paterson, T. L., M.M.	1/ 2/41
Thornton, T., (Lt. late Lothians & Border Horse)	1/ 2/41
Usher, R. J., D.S.C., (Lt.ret. R.N.)	1/ 2/41
Robertson, G. T.	8/ 5/41
Baxter, R.	22/ 6/41
Knowlson, A.	22/ 6/41

Lieutenants

Allison, T. A., (Lt. late H.L.I.)	1/ 2/41
Beattie, J. A.	1/ 2/41
Binell, R. C.	1/ 2/41
Byers, R.	1/ 2/41
Dobbie, A.	1/ 2/41

Lieutenants – contd.

Dodds, G. D., (Capt. late S. Stafford R.)	1/ 2/41
Dunlop, W. W.	1/ 2/41
Frame, J.	1/ 2/41
Grant, W. K., (Maj. T.A. Res.,	1/ 2/41
Gray, P.	1/ 2/41
Hamilton, T.	1/ 2/41
Herd, W. M., M.M.	1/ 2/41
Jardine, C.	1/ 2/41
Miller, F. M., (Lt. late K.O.Y.L.I.)	1/ 2/41
Oliver, T. B.	1/ 2/41
Rae, J., (P/O late R.A.F.)	1/ 2/41
Rae, J.	1/ 2/41
Redpath, W., (2/Lt. late R.A.)	1/ 2/41
Redpath, N. M.	1/ 2/41
Roth, W. C.	1/ 2/41
Rutherford, G.	1/ 2/41
Scott, C.	1/ 2/41
Douglas, G. G.	1/ 2/41
Fraser, G.	21/ 6/41
Burnet, W.	21/ 7/41

Adjutant & Quarter-Master

Audis, Lt., E. J., Gen. List Inf.	25/ 3/41

Medical-Officer

56455-3(64)

2nd SCOTTISH BORDER BATTALION

Lt.-Colonel

Murray, C. A. G. O., D.S.O.,
(Col. ret. pay) — 1/ 2/41

Majors

Cochran, A. C. P., (Lt.-Col.
late Ind. Army) — 1/ 2/41
Grant, G. L. — 1/ 2/41
Harrison, J., (Capt. late
K.O.S.B.) — 1/ 2/41
Marshall, A., D.S.O., (Lt.
Col. late R.F.C.) — 1/ 2/41
Rutherford, W. D., (Maj. late
K.O.S.B.) — 1/ 2/41
Thorburn, M. M., M.C., (Lt.-Col.
late K.O.S.B.) — 1/ 2/41

Captains

Danford, B. W. Y., D.S.O., (Col.
late R.E.) — 1/ 2/41
Glegg, A. C. — 1/ 2/41
Keir, J. H. — 1/ 2/41
Watson, G. — 1/ 2/41
Yarrow, K. G., (Lt. late
R.A.S.C.) — 1/ 2/41

Lieutenants

Anderson, W. — 1/ 2/41
Brown, T. S., (Lt. late
K.O.S.B.) — 1/ 2/41
Cowan, A. G., (Maj. late T.A.) — 1/ 2/41
Dryden, W. H., (Lt. late
R.G.A.) — 1/ 2/41
Hannah, E. T. R. (Lt. late
H.L.I.) — 1/ 2/41
Holmes, J. P. — 1/ 2/41
Hood, J. D. — 1/ 2/41
Jardine, J. B., C.M.G., D.S.O.,
(Hon. Brig.-Gen. ret. pay) — 1/ 2/41
Johnson, W. M. — 1/ 2/41
Johnstone, R. A. — 1/ 2/41

Lieutenants - contd.

Johnstone, R. H., (2/Lt. late
R. Scots) — 1/ 2/41
Ker, R. D., (Lt. late
K.O.S.B.) — 1/ 2/41
Little, J. R. — 1/ 2/41
Logan, H. N., (Lt. late
K.O.S.B.) — 1/ 2/41
McCreath, J. F. — 1/ 2/41
Ogilvie, G. T. A. — 1/ 2/41
Paterson, W. S. — 1/ 2/41
Robertson, A. — 1/ 2/41
Sankey, G. H. — 1/ 2/41
Silver, H. — 1/ 2/41
Stark, R. G. — 1/ 2/41
Weir, C. D. W. — 1/ 2/41
Wilson, G. T., M.C., (Lt.
late Black Watch) — 1/ 2/41
Wotton, J. H. G. — 1/ 2/41

2nd Lieutenants

Smith, D. L. — 1/ 2/41
Common, A. L. — 1/ 2/41
Laurie, A. — 1/ 2/41
McIntyre, R. J. — 1/ 2/41
Plummer, C. A. S., (Lt. late
T.A. Res.) — 1/ 2/41
Rankine, J. C. N. — 1/ 2/41
Reid, A. — 1/ 2/41
Sprott, M., (Capt. late
The Greys) — 1/ 2/41
Scott, A. G. — 4/ 7/41
Hay, J. W. (Capt. late Ind.
Army) — 8/ 7/41

Adjutant & Quarter-Master

Andrews, Capt. (actg. 1/2/41)
L. O. Gen. List Inf. — 1/ 2/41

Medical Officer

Veitch, Maj., I. D., M.B. — 1/ 2/41

91

3rd SCOTTISH BORDER BATTALION

Lt.-Colonel	
Chenevix-Trench, J. F., D.S.O. (Lt.-Col. ret. pay)	1/ 2/41

Majors	
Appleby, T., (Capt. late R. North'd Fus.)	1/ 2/41
Caley, D. C., (Capt. late M.G. Corps)	1/ 2/41
Currie, J. H., (Lt. late A. & S.H.)	1/ 2/41
Falconer, H. C., (2/Lt. late T.A.)	1/ 2/41
Henry, W. R. P., (Lt.-Col. late Ind. Army)	1/ 2/41
Inch, W., (Lt. late Can. Mil. Forces)	1/ 2/41
Munro, D. S. G., M.C., (Maj. late M.G. Corps)	1/ 2/41
White, A., (Capt. late R. War R.)	1/ 2/41
Horne, W. M. L., (Lt.-Col. late K.O.S.B.)	1/ 8/41

Captains	
Cameron, R. C., (2/Lt. ret.)	1/ 2/41
Cowan, H. H., (Lt. late R.E.)	1/ 2/41
Houston, J. L., (Capt. late K.O.S.B.)	1/ 2/41
Renton, L.	1/ 2/41
Thomson, M. S.	1/ 2/41
Sanderson, D. H.	1/ 2/41
Hay, J McM.	24/ 5/41

Lieutenants	
Brackenbury, C. H.	1/ 2/41
Bruce, J. C.	1/ 2/41
Buckle, T. F.	1/ 2/41
Church, J. C.	1/ 2/41
Cockburn, G.	1/ 2/41
Cookson, H.	1/ 2/41
Cunningham, A. U.	1/ 2/41
Elliot, F.	1/ 2/41
Forrest, R. L.	1/ 2/41
Gillon, A., (Lt.-Col. late H.L.I.)	1/ 2/41

56/455-3(66)

Lieutenants - contd.	
Hogg, A. S.	1/ 2/41
Hogg, J., (2/Lt. K.O.S.B.)	1/ 2/41
Johnston, J. M., (2/Lt. late Black Watch)	1/ 2/41
Leighton, W. H.	1/ 2/41
Little, A. R.	1/ 2/41
McDougal, G.	1/ 2/41
MacGregor, J., (2/Lt. late H.L.I.)	1/ 2/41
McKerrow, M.	1/ 2/41
Mather, J.	1/ 2/41
Mitchell, J.	1/ 2/41
Prentice, W. B., (2/Lt. late R.G.A.)	1/ 2/41
Rose, H.	1/ 2/41
Shed, A.	1/ 2/41
Thomson, R. A.	1/ 2/41
Tindal, A. G.	1/ 2/41
Walker, J. M., M.C., (Lt. late Rifle Bde.)	1/ 2/41
Whitelaw, A.	1/ 2/41
Wood, J.	1/ 2/41
Milne, D. S.	1/ 2/41
White, A.	1/ 2/41
Voase, C.	1/ 2/41
Davidson, R. M.	1/ 2/41
Duns, W.	1/ 2/41

2nd Lieutenants	
Adam, G.	1/ 2/41
Swan, D. K.	1/ 2/41
Watson, R.	1/ 2/41
Calder, D. F.	1/ 2/41
Calder, J. R.	1/ 2/41

Adjutant & Quarter-Master	
Shewen, Capt. W. G. M. K.O.S.B.)	3/ 3/41

Medical Officer	
Innes. Maj., W. M., M.B., (Capt. late T.A.)	1/ 2/41

4th SCOTTISH BORDER BATTALION

Lt.-Colonel

Stirling-Cookson, C. S., D.S.O.,
  M.C. (Bt.-Col. late T.A.)   1/ 2/41

Majors

Anderson, C., D.S.O., M.C.,
  (Maj. late R. Scots)   1/ 2/41
Bowman, D., (Capt. late R.A.)   1/ 2/41
Darling, R. S., (Maj. late
  T.A.)   1/ 2/41
Inglis, J., (Capt. late T.A.)   1/ 2/41
Laing, J. T., (2/Lt. late T.A.)   1/ 2/41
Laing, T.   1/ 2/41
Leadbetter, J. G. G., M.C.,
  (Maj. late T.A.)   1/ 2/41
Marshall, A. C., (Maj. late
  T.A.)   1/ 2/41
Sebright, J. H. K., (Capt.
  late Durham L.I.)   1/ 2/41

Captains

Aikman, J. S., M.C., (Capt.
  late A. & S.H.)   1/ 2/41
Bell, J. K.   1/ 2/41
Fraser, H., (2/Lt. late
  K.O.S.B.)   1/ 2/41
Hogarth, R. R., (Capt. late
  Lovat Scouts)   1/ 2/41
Hunter, W. C., (Lt. late R.E.)   1/ 2/41
Keith, N. W.   1/ 2/41
Scott, J. C.   1/ 2/41

Lieutenants

Bruce, J. W., (2/Lt. late T.A.)   1/ 2/41
Compton, P.   1/ 2/41
Cox, T. H. C., (Capt. late
  Black Watch)   1/ 2/41
Dryden, T., (Sub.-Lt. late
  R.N.V.R.)   1/ 2/41
Elliot, T. R., (Lt. late King's
  Own R.)   1/ 2/41
Gardiner, G.   1/ 2/41
Halliburton, W. T.   1/ 2/41
Jamieson, J.   1/ 2/41
Johnston, I. S., M.C.,
  (Capt. late R.F.A.)   1/ 2/41
Laing, W.   1/ 2/41
Maben, J., (Lt. late K.O.S.B.)   1/ 2/41
MacDuff, W. A., (Lt. late
  T.A.)   1/ 2/41
Partington, J., (2/Lt. late
  R.A.F.)   1/ 2/41
Pettigrew, A. M.   1/ 2/41
Roberton, R. J.   1/ 2/41
Scott, C. D.   1/ 2/41
Smith, T. W.   1/ 2/41
Stark, A.   1/ 2/41
Telford, R.   1/ 2/41

Lieutenants - contd.

Tudhope, A. D.   1/ 2/41
Watson, J., D.C.M.   1/ 2/41
Wight, J.   1/ 2/41
Makins, A. (2/Lt. late R.A.F.)   18/ 7/41
Hedley-Dent, P. G. H.   25/ 7/41

2nd Lieutenants

Laing, R. W.   1/ 2/41
Ogilvie, E. A., (Capt. late
  R.E.)   1/ 2/41
Paton, G. C., (Capt. late
  T.A.)   1/ 2/41
Roberton, J. S.   1/ 2/41

Adjutant & Quarter-Master

Reid, Capt. (actg. 12/5/41) W.,
  Gen. List Inf.   12/ 5/41

Medical Officer

Brown, Maj., W., O.B.E., M.B.,
  F.R.C.P. (Lt.-Col. late T.A.)   1/ 2/41

EDINBURGH UNIVERSITY S.T.C. COMPANY

Territorial Army Association }
  administering   }

City of Edinburgh T.A. Association,
  19, Palmerston Place,
  Edinburgh.

L.M.S. COMPANY (6th CITY OF EDINBURGH BATTALION)

STUDENTS MOBILE COMPANY

Lieutenant

King, A. S.   11/ 7/41

2nd Lieutenant

Drummond, K.   11/ 7/41

EDINBURGH AREA - contd.

SCOTTISH REGION (POST OFFICE) ZONE

Commander   Carter, Col. H., T.D.,
                                     (Col. T.A.)   1/ 2/41

Second-in-Command   Campbell, Lt.-Col. T., O.B.E.,
                                     (Capt. late R.E.)   1/ 2/41

Assistant Zone Commander   Yule, Maj., W., O.B.E.   1/ 2/41

Signal Officer   Horn, Maj., C. O.   1/ 2/41

Territorial Army Association   ⎤   City of Edinburgh T.A. Association,
                              ⎬   19, Palmerston Place,
    administering   ⎦   Edinburgh

56455-3(68)

GLASGOW AREA

| General Staff Officer, 1st grade | Colville, Col. (temp. 8/1/41)
Rt. Hon. D. J., T.D., M.P., T.A.
Res., t.a. | 8/ 7/40 |

NO.1 ZONE (GLASGOW)

Commander	Simpson, Col. C. S., D.S.O., T.D., (Lt.-Col. ret. T.A.)	1/ 2/41
Staff Officer	Donaldson, Capt., A. H.	1/ 2/41
Weapon Training Officer	Mathieson, Capt., H. M., (Capt. late M.G. Corps)	1/ 2/41
Transport Officer	Wilson, Lt. A.	1/ 2/41
Signal Officer	Speirs, Capt. H. McA.	23/ 7/41
Territorial Army Association administering	The City of Glasgow T.A. Association, 201, West George Street, Glasgow, C.2.	

GROUP NO.1

Commander	Reid, Col. F. W., M.C., T.D., (Maj. ret. T.A.)	1/ 2/41
Intelligence Officers	Wallace, Capt. T. W. (Lt. late R. Scots)	1/ 2/41
	Macfarlane, Capt., W., D.S.O., (Col. late T.A.)	5/ 6/41
	Meyer, Capt. A. C.	6/ 6/41
Chief Guide	Henderson, Capt., W. A., (Maj. late T.A.)	5/ 6/41
Chief Staff Officer	Barclay, Maj. J. (Capt. late R. Signals)	7/ 5/41

1st CITY OF GLASGOW BATTALION

Lt.-Colonel
Watson, E., M.C., T.D.,
(Maj. ret. T.A.)   1/ 2/41

Captains - contd.
Smith, J., (Lt. late M.G.
Corps)   1/ 2/41
Bell, S. H., (Lt. late M.G.
Corps)   1/ 2/41

Majors
Ker, R. MacN. (Maj. late
M.G. Corps)   1/ 2/41
Thomson, R. N., (Capt.
late T.A.)   1/ 2/41
Lindsay, M., (Capt. late
T.A.)   1/ 2/41
Longmuir, J. B., M.B.E.,
(Lt. late T.A.)   1/ 2/41
Cunninghame, S. S., (2/Lt.
late T.A.)   1/ 2/41
Macfarlane, P. C., T.D.,
(Bt.-Col. late T.A.)   1/ 2/41
Dowie, A. M., (Capt. late
M.G. Corps)   1/ 2/41
Parkhouse, C. E. D., (Lt. late
S. Wales Bord.)   1/ 2/41

Lieutenants
Forrest, J. E., (Capt. late
T.A.)   1/ 2/41
Hotchkiss, J. H. W., M.C.,
(Capt. late Border R.)   1/ 2/41
Barclay, J. K., (Lt. late
R.A.)   1/ 2/41
Salmond, A. B.   1/ 2/41
Pitt, J.   1/ 2/41
Macdonald, A. J., (Capt.
late Ind. Army)   1/ 2/41
Westlands, R.   1/ 2/41
Anderson, J. B., (Capt. late
Cameronians)   1/ 2/41
Paterson, A. R. B.   1/ 2/41
Miller, J., M.B.E. (Lt.
late R.E.)   1/ 2/41
Gemmill, A., (Lt. late
Cameronians)   1/ 2/41
McCormick, W. H.   1/ 2/41
Davidson, A., M.M.,
(2/Lt. late T.A.)   1/ 2/41
Fraser, G. B., (2/Lt. late
R.S. Fus.)   1/ 2/41
Gilchrist, J. A., (F/Lt.
late R.A.F.)   1/ 2/41
Marr, W. H.   1/ 2/41
Aspin, J.   1/ 2/41
Macgregor, F. M., (Capt.
late T.A.)   1/ 2/41

Captains
Kingett, A. E., (Capt. late
Ind. Army)   1/ 2/41
Stewart, A. B., (Capt. late
T.A.)   1/ 2/41
Winchester, H. W., M.C.,
(Capt. late R. Scots)   1/ 2/41
Paterson, G., (Capt. late
T.A.)   1/ 2/41

1st City of Glasgow Battalion - contd.

Lieutenants - contd.

Mackay, H. O., (2/Lt. late Black Watch)	1/ 2/41
Thaw, J.	1/ 2/41
Nunneley, R. M. C.	1/ 2/41
Morrison, J., (2/Lt. late H.L.I.)	1/ 2/41
Edmonstone, A. C., (Lt. Res. of Off.)	1/ 2/41
Gray, J., M.C., (Capt. late R.E.)	1/ 2/41
Lewis, R., D.C.M.	1/ 2/41
Tulloch, R. M., M.M., (Lt. late M.G. Corps)	1/ 2/41
McNish, P. F.	1/ 2/41
Scott, J., M.M.	1/ 2/41
Reid, W.	1/ 2/41
Brown, E. J.	1/ 2/41
Evan, J. S.	1/ 2/41
Hanley, J.	1/ 2/41
Clark, M. J., (2/Lt. late R.A.F.)	1/ 2/41
Innes, G. J., (Capt. late Scot. Rif.)	1/ 2/41
Buchanan, A. W.	18/ 7/41
Ritchie, D., (2/Lt. late R.F.A.)	18/ 7/41
Guy, J.	18/ 7/41
Stiven, J. S.	18/ 7/41

2nd Lieutenants

Morrison, J. C.	1/ 2/41
Chalmers, J. B.	1/ 2/41
Ritchie, J.	1/ 2/41
Smith, H. G., M.C., (Capt. late H.L.I.)	1/ 2/41
Scott, G. K., (Lt. late K.O.S.B.)	1/ 2/41
Jack, A.	1/ 2/41
Nelson, J. M.	1/ 2/41
Young, J. W.	1/ 2/41
Christie, C. S.	1/ 2/41
Robertson, D. M., (Lt. late H.L.I.)	1/ 2/41

2nd Lieutenants - contd.

Duncanson, R. K., (Lt. late K.A.R.)	1/ 2/41
Primrose, J. S. A.	1/ 2/41
Murray, A. G.	1/ 2/41
Macdonald, W. J.	1/ 2/41
Anderson, A. C. J. MacD. (Sub. Lt. late R.N.V.R.)	1/ 2/41
Clarkson, J.	1/ 2/41
Carruthers, R. B.	1/ 2/41
Wilson, T. G.	1/ 2/41
Calder, J.	1/ 2/41
Davidson, R.	1/ 2/41
Hay, W.	1/ 2/41
Murray, W. C., (Lt. late K.O.S.B.)	1/ 2/41
Little, J. R. R.	1/ 2/41
Brown, J.	1/ 2/41
McArthur, J. T.	1/ 2/41
Crawford, T. C., C.I.E.	1/ 2/41
Hill, F. G.	1/ 2/41
Hewit, J. H.	1/ 2/41
Macdonald, A.	1/ 2/41
Campbell, D.	1/ 2/41
Edgar, J., (Lt. late London Scottish)	1/ 2/41
Henry, J. P.	1/ 2/41
Strathee. G.	1/ 2/41
Walker, A., M.M.	1/ 2/41
Johnston, F. C.	1/ 2/41
Connor, E.	1/ 2/41
Gibb, R. P. F. C. R., T.D. (Bt. Col. T.A. Res.)	1/ 2/41

Adjutant & Quarter-Master

Medical Officer

Cuthbertson, Maj. D. P., M.D., (2/Lt. late R.S. Fus.)	1/ 2/41

GLASGOW AREA - contd.

NO. 1 ZONE (GLASGOW) - contd.

GROUP NO. 1 - contd.

2nd CITY OF GLASGOW BATTALION

Lt.-Colonel

Hastie, S. H,, O.B.E., M.C., (Maj. late H.L.I.)	1/ 2/41

Majors

Cotching, C. E., M.C., (Capt. late Seaforth)	1/ 2/41
Macdonald, K., (Capt. late Black Watch)	1/ 2/41
Urquhart, J. M., (Lt. late M. G. Corps.)	1/ 2/41
Lee, R. E., M.C.	1/ 2/41
Mann, J., (Capt. late Inniskilling Fus.)	1/ 2/41
Smith, D. P.	1/ 2/41
Taylor, R. D., (2/Lt. late Cameronians)	7/ 5/41

Captains

McIntosh, C., (Capt. late R.A.)	1/ 2/41
Macfarlane, J. R., M.M.	1/ 2/41
Walker, W. M.	1/ 2/41
Moller, J., M.C., (Lt. late R.A.)	1/ 2/41
Martin, A. E., (Lt. late R.A.S.C.)	
Gale, J. A., (Capt. late R.A.)	10/ 6/41

Lieutenants

Goldie, G. H.	1/ 2/41
Russell, J., (Lt. late H.L.I.)	1/ 2/41
Stewart, W. B.	1/ 2/41
Taylor, F. W., (Capt. late T.A.)	1/ 2/41
Merrylees, A. R., (Maj. late Gordons)	1/ 2/41
Stevenson, L. M., (Lt. late T.A.)	1/ 2/41
Grant, W.	1/ 2/41
Thompson, J. G.	1/ 2/41
Moore, A. A.	1/ 2/41
Rennie, T. H.	1/ 2/41
Weir, J.	1/ 2/41
King, J. A.	1/ 2/41
Waller, G. E., M.C., (Lt. late M. G. Corps)	1/ 2/41
Mackie, J.	1/ 2/41
Ramsay, D. M., M.C., (Capt. late A. & S.H.)	1/ 2/41
Flinn, E. C.	1/ 2/41
Bishop, H.	1/ 2/41
Russell, T. B.	1/ 2/41
Hay, A. H.	1/ 2/41
Hutton, D. A., (Capt. late R.E.)	1/ 2/41

Lieutenants - contd.

Londen, L. M.	1/ 2/41
Duncanson, J.	1/ 2/41
Rolla, J.	10/ 6/41
Marshall, J.	10/ 6/41
Findlay,. W. S.	10/ 6/41
McMillan, P. S.	17/ 6/41
McMorran, J.	1/ 7/41
Young, T.	1/ 7/41
Gillon, J. T.	21/ 7/41
Kerr, D. M.	21/ 7/41
Campbell, L. H.	21/ 7/41

2nd Lieutenants

Seymour, H.	1/ 2/41
Watson, A. D.	1/ 2/41
McKinnon, J., (Lt. late A. & S.H.)	1/ 2/41
McLetchie, A. B.	1/ 2/41
Lewis, M. R., (Lt. late T.A.)	1/ 2/41
Johnston, A.	1/ 2/41
Macdonald, A.	1/ 2/41
Haggarty, H.	1/ 2/41
Hamilton, A. G., (Lt. late R.F.A.)	1/ 2/41
Crawford, P. C.	1/ 2/41
Towers, W., D.C.M., M.M.	1/ 2/41
Ross, W. C., (Capt. late A. & S.H.)	1/ 2/41
Graham, W., (2/Lt. late R.A.F.)	1/ 2/41
MacCormick, J. M.	1/ 2/41
Moodie, J. M.	1/ 2/41
Bonellie, C. B.	1/ 2/41
Mitchell, D. K.	1/ 2/41
Walker, J.	1/ 2/41
Law, J.	1/ 2/41
Davidson, H.	1/ 2/41

Adjutant & Quarter-Master

Medical Officer

Peacock, Maj. P. R.	1/ 7/41

GLASGOW AREA - contd.

NO. 1 ZONE (GLASGOW) - contd.

GROUP NO. 1 - contd.

6th CITY OF GLASGOW BATTALION

Lt.-Colonel
Macdonald, N., T.D., (Lt.-Col.   1/ 2/41
  T.A. Res.)

Majors
McBeath, W. J., M.C., D.C.M.,   1/ 2/41
  (Capt. late H.L.I.)
Hall, W. M.   1/ 2/41
Murray, R., (Capt. late Gordons) 1/ 2/41
Bujnowski, A., M.C., (Lt. late   1/ 2/41
  Seaforth)
Lang, I. S. M., (Capt. late   1/ 2/41
  R.F.A.)
Horne, W. W., M.C., (Capt. late 1/ 2/41
  K.O.S.B.)

Captains
Cameron, J.   1/ 2/41
Blackley, J., (Lt. late H.L.I.) 1/ 2/41
Man, J. S.   1/ 2/41
Scaife, W.   1/ 2/41

Lieutenants
Elliot, J.   1/ 2/41
Buchanan J.   1/ 2/41
Pattison, D. M., M.M., (Lt.   1/ 2/41
  late R.E.)
McCorkindale, J. A., (2/Lt.   1/ 2/41
  late K.O.S.B.)
Seely, C. L.   1/ 2/41
Kinnear, J., (Lt. late H.L.I.) 1/ 2/41
Thomson, C. F.   1/ 2/41
Ferguson, J., (Lt. late R.E.) 1/ 2/41
Ewen, R. D.   1/ 2/41
Macleod, J., D.C.M.   1/ 2/41
Mowat, J., D.C.M., M.M.   1/ 2/41
Sweeting, J.   1/ 2/41
Davidson, J., M.M.   1/ 2/41
Currie, T.   1/ 2/41
Gray, A. F., M.M.   1/ 2/41
Gray, T.   1/ 2/41
McCallum, J.   1/ 2/41
Gardner, J.   1/ 2/41
Macfarlane, W. B.   1/ 2/41
Jamieson, E. A.   1/ 2/41

Lieutenants - contd.
Brown, J. G.   1/ 2/41
Gilmour, A.   1/ 2/41
Chalmers, J. S., (2/Lt. late   1/ 2/41
  H.L.I.)
Young, J. M.   1/ 2/41
Irvine, W. B.   1/ 2/41
Hill, S.   1/ 2/41
Ewing, J., (2/Lt. late R.A.F.) 1/ 2/41
Stirling, J.   1/ 2/41
Simonsen, K. K.   1/ 2/41
McConnell, A. M.   1/ 2/41
Turner, E. A.   1/ 2/41
Murray, A. L.   1/ 2/41
Dallas, G., (Capt. late R.G.A.) 1/ 2/41

2nd Lieutenants
Wilson, T.   1/ 2/41
Stalker, J.   1/ 2/41
Evans, F.   1/ 2/41
Blyth, J.   1/ 2/41
Maclaghlan, S. D. L.   1/ 2/41
Miller, W. M.   1/ 2/41
Macewan, V. V.   1/ 2/41
Mackenzie, J. S.   1/ 2/41
Smith, J.   1/ 2/41
Dye, J. W.   1/ 2/41
Walker, T.   21/ 5/41
McConachy, J. McA.   3/ 6/41
Cameron, A.   3/ 6/41
Hobbs, D. E.   3/ 6/41
Pollock, A. G.   3/ 6/41
Mackellar, J.   11/ 6/41
Forrest, T. M.   20/ 6/41
Brodie, S. H., M.M.   28/ 6/41
Campbell, A.   28/ 6/41

Adjutant & Quarter-Master

Medical Officer

GLASGOW AREA – contd.

NO. 1 ZONE (GLASGOW) – contd.

GROUP NO. 2

Commander	Bagley, Col. E. H., T.D., (Bt.-Col. ret. T.A.	1/ 2/4
Staff Officer (G)	Ford, Maj., W., (Lt. late M.G. Corps)	17/ 6/4
Staff Officer	McGregor, Capt., D. (Lt. late Cameronians)	1/ 2/4

3rd CITY OF GLASGOW BATTALION

Lt.-Colonel

Ogg, G. J., (Lt. late T.A.)	1/ 2/41

Majors

McGregor, A., (Lt. late M.G. Corps.)	1/ 2/41
Jackson, J. B. McI.	1/ 2/41
McIntosh, H., M.C., (Capt. late A. & S.H.)	1/ 2/41
Bell, H. H.	1/ 2/41
Robertson, J., (2/Lt. late R.A.S.C.)	1/ 2/41
Patterson, H. F., (Capt. late Cameronian)	28/ 5/41
Hart, E. R.	18/ 6/41
Gillespie, E., (Capt. late K.O.S.B.)	18/ 6/41

Captains

Fleming, J.	1/ 2/41
Mackenzie, T. B.	1/ 2/41
Hutton, R. C., (2/Lt. late T.A.)	18/ 6/41
Kerr, J. C., (Capt. late Ind. Army)	18/ 6/41
Scutar, M. W. (Lt. late R. Scots.)	18/ 6/41
Gibson, R.	19/ 6/41
Wood, G., (Lt. late R.A.)	23/ 7/41

Lieutenants

Muir, G. S., M.M.	1/ 2/41
Cauld, J. T.	1/ 2/41
Jack, R. D.	1/ 2/41
Braidwood, J. R.	1/ 2/41
Findlay, J.	1/ 2/41
Rolland, R. A.	1/ 2/41

Lieutenants–contd.

Macgregor, E. P.	1/ 2/4
Harkness, W. B.	1/ 2/4
Muir, J.	1/ 2/4
Sinclair, H. Mac. N.	1/ 2/4
Martin, A.	1/ 2/4
Kerr, A.	18/ 6/4
Wilkie, J. M.	18/ 6/4
Kelly, W. E., M.C. (Capt. late Border R.)	18/ 6/4

2nd Lieutenants

Haining, G. A., M.C., (Lt. late K.O.S.B.)	1/ 2/4
Millar, B. J.	1/ 2/4
Pearson, A. B., (Lt. late H.L.I.)	1/ 2/4
Wilson, D.	1/ 2/4
Arnott, W.	1/ 2/4
Hamilton, A. S., (Lt. late Cameronians (S.R.))	1/ 2/4
Brownlie, J. McH.	1/ 2/4
Brewis, J. A., (Lt. late R. Lancs. R.)	10/ 6/4
Stewart, H. S.	10/ 6/4
Medlock, C. M., (2/Lt. late Seaforth)	18/ 6/4

Adjutant & Quarter-Master

Medical Officer

Grant, Maj. I. D., (Capt. late Ind. Med. Serv.)	1/ 2/4

GLASGOW AREA – **contd.**

NO. 1 ZONE (GLASGOW) – **contd.**

GROUP NO. 2 – contd.

11th CITY OF GLASGOW BATTALION

Lt.-Colonel
Walden, R. F., (Capt. ret. pay)   1/ 2/41

Majors
Maclean, J. A. S., (Capt. late   1/ 2/41
T.A.)
Paton, J. W.   1/ 2/41
Whitam, L.   1/ 2/41
Glen, A. G., (Lt. late T.A.)   1/ 2/41
Osborne, F. H., (Lt. late   1/ 2/41
R.A.F.)

Captains
Cunningham, C.   1/ 2/41
Keppie, G., (Lt. late R.A.)   1/ 2/41
Taylor, G., M.M.   1/ 2/41
Roxburgh, J., (Capt. late R.A.)   1/ 2/41
Fleming, W. R., M.M.   1/ 2/41
Miln, D. C.   1/ 2/41

Lieutenants
Dykes, G.   1/ 2/41
Henderson, J., M.C., (Capt.   1/ 2/41
late R.T.R.)
Hair, D. K.,   1/ 2/41
Gilchrist, A. A., (Capt. late   1/ 2/41
T.A.)
Marskell, W. G.   1/ 2/41
Lockhead, A.   1/ 2/41
Hutton, C. M.   1/ 2/41
Stevenson, J. B.   1/ 2/41

Lieutenants–contd.
Collins, W.   1/ 2/41
Allan, D. H.   1/ 2/41
Thomson, A. J. I.   1/ 2/41
Gillies, A.   1/ 2/41
Stevens, J.   1/ 2/41
Espie, A.   1/ 2/41
Paterson, R.E.   1/ 2/41
Langley, J. S.   1/ 2/41
Aitchison, J. G.   1/ 2/41
Dalgarno, J. D.   1/ 2/41
Fiddes, A., M.M.   1/ 2/41

2nd Lieutenants
Hair, J. M.   1/ 2/41
Storrie, W.   1/ 2/41
McWilliam, J. S.   1/ 2/41
Guild, J.   1/ 2/41
Goulding, J. S.   1/ 2/41
Wilson, H. W.   1/ 2/41
Wallace, G. A. L.   1/ 2/41
Allen, H.   1/ 2/41
Welsh, N. M.   1/ 2/41
Colville, W. I.   1/ 2/41
Craig, D. R.   1/ 2/41
Mitchell, A.   1/ 2/41

Adjutant & Quarter-Master

Medical Officer

GLASGOW AREA - contd.

NO. 1 ZONE (GLASGOW) - contd.

GROUP NO. 3

Commander	Sayers, Col., D. H., M.C., (Capt. late T.A. 1/ 2/4
Staff Officer	Dobie, Maj. W.S.C. (Lt. late T.A.)5/ 6/4

7th CITY OF GLASGOW (L.M.S. RAILWAY) BATTALION

Lt.-Colonel
Killin, J., (Capt. late T.A.)   1/ 2/41

Majors
Strachan, G. N.   1/ 2/41
Simpson, R.   1/ 2/41
Dalglish, W. McC., M.M.   1/ 2/41
Anderson, C. W.   1/ 2/41
Barclay, C. W.   1/ 2/41
Ballantyne, J. C.   1/ 2/41
Sneddon, T. D.   1/ 2/41

Captains
Fowell, R. J.   1/ 2/41
Walker, N. M., M.M.   1/ 2/41
Joyce, J.   1/ 2/41
McLean, A., M.C., (2/Lt. late R. Fus.)   1/ 2/41
Sloan, J. R. L.   1/ 2/41

Lieutenants
Welsh, J. S.   1/ 2/41
Stirling, A.   1/ 2/41
Stark, W.   1/ 2/41
Houston, R.   1/ 2/41
Jamieson, D. T.   1/ 2/41
Campbell, J. G.   1/ 2/41
Calder, J. N.   1/ 2/41
Gardner, W.   1/ 2/41
Wylie, D. C.   1/ 2/41
Clark, J.   1/ 2/41
McMaster, J.   1/ 2/41
Sandilands, C.   1/ 2/41
Sandison, F. W.   1/ 2/41
Macandie, H.   1" 2/41
Gall, A. M.   1/ 2/41
Lamont, A. M.   1/ 2/41
Galbraith, J.   1/ 2/41
Middleton, W.   1/ 2/41
Sinclair, J.   1/ 2/41

Lieutenants - contd.
Treadgold, G. A., (2/Lt. late R.A.F.)   1/ 2/4
Hearns, G.   1/ 2/4
Stirling, R. P. M.   1/ 2/4
Newman, J.   1/ 2/4
Hall, J. B.   22/ 5/4

2nd Lieutenants
Maguire, J. B.   1/ 2/4
Irvine, D. C.   1/ 2/4
Gibson, J. A. B.   1/ 2/4
Stirling, R. P. M.   1/ 2/4
Melville, A.   1/ 2/4
Thomson, J.   1/ 2/4
Murdoch, R.   1/ 2/4
Donaldson, P.   1/ 2/4
Richmond, W.   1/ 2/4
Cliff, F. A.   1/ 2/4
McLeod, J. H.   1/ 2/4
Caldow, G. L.   1/ 2/4
Saunders, T.   1/ 2/4
Binnie, A., (Capt. late R.A.F.)   1/ 2/4
Beveridge, P.   1/ 2/4
Paterson, J.   1/ 2/4
Martin, D.   1/ 2/4
Little, D.   1/ 2/4
Rutherford, J.   1/ 2/4
Jackson, T.   1/ 2/4
Coutts, A. H. S.   1/ 2/4
Beattie, R.   1/ 2/4

Adjutant & Quarter-Master

Medical Officer
Watt, Maj., T.C.D., M.C., M.B., (Maj. late R.A.M.C.)   1/ 2/

GLASGOW AREA - contd.

No. 1 ZONE (GLASGOW) - contd.

No. 3 GROUP - contd.

8th CITY OF GLASGOW (L.N.E.R) BATTALION

Lt.-Colonel
Underwood, W. H.   1/ 2/41

Majors
Smart, H. F.   1/ 2/41
Fleming, J.   1/ 2/41
Leigh, C.   1/ 2/41
Renwick, R. A. M., D.C.M.   1/ 2/41
Hawkes, T. R.   1/ 2/41
Strachan, W. M.M.   1/ 2/41
Brown, A. R.   1/ 2/41

Captains
Meara, L.   1/ 2/41
Bennett, J.   1/ 2/41
Burkitt, J., M.M.   1/ 2/41
Wilkinson, T. F., M.M.   1/ 2/41
Perry, H. J. B., (Lt. late
  R.N.R.)   1/ 2/41
Bilsland, W.   1/ 2/41
Roberts, D., M.M.   21/ 5/41

Lieutenants
Raw, P. G.   1/ 2/41
Haveron, D.   1/ 2/41
Macfarlane, R.   1/ 2/41
Oldham, R.   1/ 2/41
Laing, D.   1/ 2/41
Hill, D.   1/ 2/41
Brown, J. J. S.   1/ 2/41
Letham, W. L.   1/ 2/41
Fergusson, R.   1/ 2/41
Ferguson, C. S.   1/ 2/41
Alexander, J. C.   1/ 2/41
Cockburn, T.   1/ 2/41
Wilson, J. M.   1/ 2/41

Lieutenants - contd.
Hasty, H. W.   1/ 2/41
Baikie, W. D.   1/ 2/41
Turnbull, G.   1/ 2/41
Parker, A. C.   1/ 2/41
Drummond, A. C. W.   1/ 2/41
Sirrie, E.   1/ 2/41
Duffus, J.   1/ 2/41
Garden, R. L.   1/ 2/41

2nd Lieutenants
Greig, W.   1/ 2/41
Wilkinson, A. F.   1/ 2/41
Ross, A. F.   1/ 2/41
Taylor, A.   1/ 2/41
Miller, J.   1/ 2/41
Brown, A. G.   1/ 2/41
Grindlay, M.   1/ 2/41
Neill, J. K.   1/ 2/41
Glen, W.   1/ 2/41
Callander, A.   1/ 2/41
Oatts, H. H.   1/ 2/41
Bassett, M. J. B.   1/ 2/41
Mackintosh, R. G. A.   1/ 2/41
Crompton, C. M. Y., D.S.O.,
  (Lt./Cmdr. R.N.)   1/ 2/41
Baird, J. M.M.   1/ 2/41
Shields, P. S.   1/ 2/41

Adjutant & Quarter-Master

Medical Officer
van Bavel, Maj. H. G. J., M.B.,
  (Maj. late R.A.M.C.)   1/ 2/41

GLASGOW AREA - contd.

No. 1 ZONE (GLASGOW) - contd.

GROUP No. 4

Commander	Mickel, Col. A., (Capt. late R.E.)	1/ 2/41
Second-in-Command	Craig, Lt.-Col., A., (Capt. late K.A.R:)	1/ 2/41
Intelligence Officer	Satterford, Capt., P. T.	1/ 2/41

4th CITY OF GLASGOW BATTALION

Lt.-Colonel

Boyd, J.	1/ 2/41

Majors

James, J., (Maj. late R.E.)	1/ 2/41
Friend, S., (Capt. late R.A.)	1/ 2/41
Waddell, R. B., (Capt. late R.A.)	1/ 2/41
Grant, T. D., (Capt. late T.A.)	1/ 2/41
Stewart, Sir James W., Bt., (Lt. late R.A.)	1/ 2/41
Ward, T. K., (Lt. late M.G.Corps)	1/ 2/41

Captains

Nithsdale, W., (2/Lt. late R.A.F.)	1/ 2/41
Smith, R. M., (Lt. late H.L.I.)	1/ 2/41
Cook, S.	1/ 2/41
Borthwick, R. J., (Capt. late T.A.)	1/ 2/41
Weir, J. D., (Lt. late R.A.)	1/ 2/41
Riddell, J. F.	1/ 2/41
Mitchell, A. R., M.C., (2/Lt. late T.A.)	1/ 2/41
Gilchrist, J., (late T.A. Res.)	1/ 2/41

Lieutenants

Samuel, J. M.	1/ 2/41
Batchelor, F., (Lt. late Black Watch)	1/ 2/41
Dawson, T. P.	1/ 2/41
Muir, R. A.	1/ 2/41
Scott, J.	1/ 2/41
Gray, T. D., (Lt. late T.A.)	1/ 2/41
Sharp, R. S.	1/ 2/41
Macmillan, M. G., M.M.	1/ 2/41
Adam, D., (Capt. late Camerons)	1/ 2/41
Stewart, H. A. V., M.M.	1/ 2/41
Jeffrey, J.	1/ 2/41
Robertson, W. A., M.C., (Lt. late R.N.V.R.)	1/ 2/41
Michael, T. G.	1/ 2/41
Halley, G. B. (Capt. T.A. Res.)	1/ 2/41
Crawford, J.	1/ 2/41
Blaber, C. E. F.	1/ 2/41
Lawson, W. M., (Lt. late H.L.I.)	1/ 2/41
Wilson, A. H.	1/ 2/41
Strachan, G.	1/ 2/41
Morton, T. A.	1/ 2/41
Drysdale, I. (2/Lt. late T.A.)	1/ 2/41
Tennant, W. W.	1/ 2/41
Gibb, J.	1/ 2/41
Whyte, A. M. (Lt. late R.S. Fus.)	1/ 2/41
Nicol, D. S.	5/ 6/41

GLASGOW AREA – contd.

No. 1 ZONE (GLASGOW) – contd.

GROUP No. 4 – contd.

4th City of Glasgow Battalion – contd.

2nd Lieutenants		Adjutant & Quarter-Master
Crush, H. C.	1/ 2/41	
Gibson, W. T.	1/ 2/41	
Drimmie, J. M.	1/ 2/41	
Beveridge, J. C.	1/ 2/41	
Smith, R.	1/ 2/41	
Taylor, W.	1/ 2/41	
Muir, D. L.	1/ 2/41	
Wright, J.	1/ 2/41	
Allen, P. S.	1/ 2/41	
Dunlop, G. K., D.C.M.,		
(Capt. T.A. Res.)	1/ 2/41	
Barradell-Smith, W.	1/ 2/41	
Chandler, F. J.	1/ 2/41	
Hammerton, E.	1/ 2/41	Medical Officer
Henderson, F., M.M.	1/ 2/41	Ashby, Maj. R. W. S., M.B.,
Galbraith, S. D.	1/ 2/41	(Lt. late K.R.R.C.) 1/ 2/41
Mackenzie, W.	1/ 2/41	
Grant, W.	1/ 2/41	
Higgins, E.	1/ 2/41	
Rae, A.	1/ 2/41	
Burns, J.	1/ 2/41	
Law, J.	1/ 2/41	
Westwood, G.	1/ 2/41	
Muir, D.	1/ 2/41	
Taylor, J. N.	1/ 2/41	
Tozer, A. H., (Lt. late		
Cheshire R.)	1/ 2/41	
Shaw, J.	1/ 2/41	
Black, D. L. R.	1/ 2/41	
Macmillan, M. G. M.M.	1/ 2/41	

GLASGOW AREA — <u>contd.</u>

No. 1 ZONE (GLASGOW) — <u>contd.</u>

GROUP No. 4 — <u>contd.</u>

5th CITY OF GLASGOW BATTALION

Lt.-Colonel

Cuthbertson, R. A., (<u>Lt. late T.A.</u>)	1/ 2/41

Majors

Hughes, A., (<u>Lt. late A. & S.H.</u>)	1/ 2/41
Bryant, F. W.	1/ 2/41
Hendrie, A. J., (<u>Capt. late H.L.I.</u>)	1/ 2/41
Lang, G. M., <u>M.C.</u>, (Capt. late H. L.I.)	1/ 2/41
Wilson, J. M., (<u>Maj. late T.A.</u>)	1/ 2/41
Harvie, R., <u>T.D.</u>, (Capt. late A. & S.H.)	1/ 2/41

Captains

Crawford, J., <u>M.B.E.</u>, (<u>Lt. late Cameronians</u>)	1/ 2/41
Hunter, R. A., (<u>Capt. late R.F.A.</u>)	1/ 2/41
Hunter, R. B.	1/ 2/41
Paterson, W.	1/ 2/41
Trail, G. J.	1/ 2/41
Allen, R. J.	1/ 2/41
Charles, D. A.	1/ 2/41
Tocher, A. D., (<u>2/Lt. late R.G.A.</u>)	1/ 2/41
Gemmell, N. L.	1/ 2/41

Captains — contd.

Hutcheon, J.	1/ 2/41
Marples, N. C., (<u>Capt. T.A. Res.</u>)	1/ 2/41
Lang, J. R., (<u>Lt.-Col. late R.A.</u>)	1/ 2/41
Lapping, R. H.	1/ 2/41
McGilp, A.	1/ 2/41

Lieutenants

Gillies, C., (<u>Lt. late Cameronians</u>)	1/ 2/41
Brodie, J.	1/ 2/41
Edmondson, A. S., (<u>2/Lt. late R.A.</u>)	1/ 2/41
Squair, R.	1/ 2/41
Tucker, W. V.	1/ 2/41
Taylor, W. M.	1/ 2/41
Peebles, J., (<u>Lt. late R.S. Fus.</u>)	1/ 2/41
Campbell, J. B.	1/ 2/41
Reid, J. M.	1/ 2/41
Henderson, W. P., (<u>2/Lt. late R. Scots</u>)	1/ 2/41
Fleming, J. T.	1/ 2/41
Sheddon, G. P., <u>D.C.M.</u>	1/ 2/41
Stewart, R., (<u>2/Lt. late Cameronians</u>)	1/ 2/41
Blackwood, D. D., <u>M.M.</u>	1/ 2/41
Bowen, J. L.	1/ 2/41
Macarthur, K.	1/ 2/41
Harding, W. A., (<u>2/Lt. late T.A.</u>)	1/ 2/41
Robertson, J. B.	1/ 2/41
Fleming, D. S.	1/ 2/41
Rae, A. M.	1/ 2/41
Haddow, A.	1/ 2/41
Ross, C.	1/ 2/41

GLASGOW AREA — contd.

NO.1 ZONE (GLASGOW) — contd.

GROUP NO.4 — contd.

5th City of Glasgow Battalion — contd.

Lieutenants — contd.

Michael, N. F.	1/ 2/41
Marshall, A. B.	1/ 2/41
Lyle, E. G., M.M.	1/ 2/41
Clark, R.	1/ 2/41
Thomson, J.	1/ 2/41
Steel, F., (2/Lt. late R.A.F.)	1/ 2/41.
Masterman, H. W.	1/ 2/41
Christie, A., (2/Lt. late H.L.I.)	1/ 2/41
Hargreaves, W.	11/ 7/41
Henderson, G. (Capt. late R.A.)	1/ 8/41

Adjutant & Quarter-Master (for Henderson, G.)

2nd Lieutenants

Allan, H.	1/ 2/41
Cunningham, D. B.	1/ 2/41
Ashby, R. J.	1/ 2/41
Murray, A. R.	1/ 2/41
Orr, R. W.	1/ 2/41
Dryman, W.	1/ 2/41
Fisher, H. J. B.	1/ 2/41
Lyle, R.	1/ 2/41
McLean, J.	1/ 2/41
McGowan, D. L.	1/ 2/41
Roy, A. W.	1/ 2/41
Watson, J., M.M.	1/ 2/41
McCredie, J. B.	1/ 2/41
Mackay, D. A., (Capt. late R.E.)	1/ 2/41
McPherson, F.	1/ 2/41
Weir, J. O.	1/ 2/41

Medical Officer
Dykes, Maj. S. N. (Capt. late R.A.M.C.)   1/ 2/41

116

12th CITY OF GLASGOW BATTALION

Lt.-Colonel

Lilley, F. J. P., (Capt. late T.A.)   1/ 2/41

Majors

Glass, R., (Lt. late Cameronians)   1/ 2/41

Renfrew, R. S., (Lt. late Gordons)   1/ 2/41

Garland, W.   1/ 2/41

Swan, N. F., (Lt. late Seaforth)   1/ 2/41

Flynn, D.   1/ 2/41

Captains

Macdonald, I. M.   1/ 2/41

Hughes, R.   1/ 2/41

McCall, T., (Lt. late T.A.)   1/ 2/41

Gallagher, W. G.   1/ 2/41

Bernard, A. C.   1/ 2/41

Dow, W. F. T.   1/ 2/41

Ritchie, T., M.M.   1/ 2/41

Snelus, E. G.   1/ 2/41

Murchie, A., (F/Lt. late R.A.F.)   1/ 2/41

Lieutenants

Murray, J. B.   1/ 2/41

Girvan, W.   1/ 2/41

Gardiner, J. P.   1/ 2/41

Young, J.   1/ 2/41

Davidson, J. A. M.   1/ 2/41

Dobson, H.   1/ 2/41

Smith, W. W.   1/ 2/41

Moir, H. C., (2/Lt. late A. & S.H.)   1/ 2/41

Ingram, C. G.   1/ 2/41

McCrone, J.   1/ 2/41

Hardie, G. M. M., D.C.M.   1/ 2/41

Macfarlane, A.   1/ 2/41

Ferguson, J. D.   1/ 2/41

Kemlo, W. H., (Lt. late A.I.F.)   1/ 2/41

Howaf., W.   1/ 2/41

Rintoul, A. (late R.N.V.R.)   1/ 2/41

Fraser, J. S., (Lt. late H.L.I.   1/ 2/41

Gibson, W. D.   1/ 2/41

Adams, J. W.   1/ 2/41

Barrie, W. G. (2/Lt. late Ind. Army)   1/ 2/41

Livingstone, D.   1/ 2/41

Cathcart, W.   1/ 2/41

McColl, J. R.   1/ 2/41

Mavor, E. I. (2/Lt. late H.L.I.)   1/ 2/41

Semple, G. A.   1/ 2/41

Paterson, C.   1/ 2/41

Bell, W. R. W. (late R.T.R.)   1/ 2/41

Fleming, J.   1/ 2/41

Taylor, J., (Capt. late T.A.)   1/ 2/41

McIntyre, W. B., M.C., (Lt. late R.G.A.)   1/ 2/41

Cunningham, J. Y., (Lt. late A. & S.H.)   1/ 2/41

McArthur, J. F.   1/ 2/41

Crawford, J. W.   1/ 2/41

Irving, R. (Sub.Lt. late R.N.A.S.)   1/ 2/41

Mayall, C.   1/ 2/41

Arthur, W., M.C., (Capt. T.A. Gen. List)   1/ 2/41

Box, F. W.   18/ 6/41

GLASGOW AREA – contd.

NO.1 ZONE (GLASGOW) – contd.

GROUP NO.4 – contd.

12th City of Glasgow Battalion – contd.

2nd Lieutenants

Primrose, J. A. M.	1/ 2/41	
Hudson, W. B.	1/ 2/41	
McCafferty, H.	1/ 2/41	
Carmichael, C., D.C.M.	1/ 2/41	
Owens, H.	1/ 2/41	Adjutant & Quarter-Master
Hamilton, J.	1/ 2/41	
McKenzie, J. B.	1/ 2/41	
Drummond, W. S.	1/ 2/41	
Ogg, F. G.	1/ 2/41	
Sommerville, A.	1/ 2/41	
Campbell, A.	1/ 2/41	
Borland, G. N., (Lt. late R.A.S.C.)	1/ 2/41	
Macfarlane, D. S.	1/ 2/41	
Livingston, A. B.	1/ 2/41	
Swanson, H. H.	1/ 2/41	
Scott, R.	1/ 2/41	
Henderson, R.	1/ 2/41	
Myers, T. McG.	1/ 2/41	
Brockett, E. A.	1/ 2/41	Medical Officer
Boothby, T. A.	1/ 2/41	Mackinnon, Maj., E. J. 1/ 2/41
Fraser, J.	1/ 2/41	
Gourlay, R.	1/ 2/41	
Low, E.	1/ 2/41	
Munro, A. McG.	1/ 2/41	
Forrester, D.	1/ 2/41	
Gow, A., (2/Lt. late H.L.I.)	1/ 2/41	
Paterson, J. McG.	1/ 2/41	
Thomson, R. G.	1/ 2/41	
Kean, D.	1/ 2/41	
Craig, J. L., (Lt. late R.G.A.)	1/ 2/41	
Stormonth, S. G.	1/ 2/41	
Little, G. W.	1/ 2/41	
Milne, W. A. P.	1/ 2/41	

GLASGOW AREA – contd.

NO. 1 ZONE (GLASGOW) – contd.

GROUP NO. 5

| Commander | Begg, Col. R. W., T.D., (Bt.-Col. ret. T.A.) | 1/ 2/41 |

GROUP NO. 6

| Commander | Bott, Col. J. G. | 1/ 2/41 |
| Zone Chief Guide | McQueen, Capt. D., (Lt. late Cameronians) | 27/ 5/41 |

9th CITY OF GLASGOW (14th GENERAL POST OFFICE) BATTALION

Majors
Martin, F. P., (In Command)	1/ 2/41
Rodger, A. B.	1/ 2/41
Masterton, J. K.	1/ 2/41
Mathie, W. H., D.C.M.	1/ 2/41

Captains
Cumming, C. R.	1/ 2/41
Bonnington, J.	1/ 2/41
Symington, G. K.	1/ 2/41
Hunter, J. D.	1/ 2/41
Brown, A.	1/ 2/41

Lieutenants
Galbraith, A.	1/ 2/41
Cree, D D. S., (Lt. late City of London R.)	1/ 2/41
McCormick, J. H.	1/ 2/41
Stewart, D. W. M., D.C M.	1/ 2/41
Adamson, G.	1/ 2/41
Gorman, T.	1/ 2/41
Johnston, J. M.	1/ 2/41
McCall, J.	1/ 2/41
McLaren, J. L.	1/ 2/41
Fraser, J U.	1/ 2/41
Stoddart, J. C.	1/ 2/41
Bedworth, A.	1/ 2/41
Groom, J. F. (2/ Lt. late R.A.F.)	1/ 2/41
Sinclair, A.	13/ 6/41
Morison, A. M.	13/ 6/41
Rowand, T	1/ 7/41
Gordon, W. J.	18/ 7/41
	1/ 2/41

2nd Lieutenants
| Campbell, J. W. | 1/ 2/41 |
| Henderson, J., (Lt. late Rifle Bde.) | 1/ 2/41 |

Adjutant & Quarter-Master
Knox, Capt. (actg. 28/4/41)
J., Gen. List Inf.   28/ 4/41

Medical Officer

GLASGOW AREA - <u>contd.</u>

NO. 1 ZONE (GLASGOW) - <u>contd.</u>

GROUP NO. 6 - <u>contd.</u>

10th CITY OF GLASGOW (15th
GENERAL POST OFFICE) BATTALION

Lt.-Colonel	
Millar, H. T. W.	1/ 2/41

Majors	
Cameron, J. (<u>Lt. late. R.E.</u>)	1/ 2/41
Knox, J.	1/ 2/41
McLean, H. H.	1/ 2/41
Stanbury, C. H.	1/ 2/41
Anderson, N. C. (<u>Lt. late</u> <u>R. Signals</u>)	1/ 2/41

Captains	
Niven, A.	1/ 2/41
Bland, F. E.	1/ 2/41
Rushbridge, E. S.	1/ 2/41
Stewart, J.	1/ 2/41
Henderson, J. R.	1/ 2/41
McCrowther, J. E. S.	1/ 2/41
Hill, A.	1/ 2/41
Watson, J.	1/ 2/41
Hunter, G.	1/ 2/41
McCall, W. (<u>Capt. late T.A.</u>)	1/ 2/41

Lieutenants	
Cameron, A.	1/ 2/41
Brierton, A. H.	1/ 2/41
McIntyre, W. G.	1/ 2/41
Wilson, J.	1/ 2/41
Keith, E.	1/ 2/41
Marshall, D. E.	1/ 2/41
Young, F. C.	1/ 2/41
Kirkpatrick, G.	1/ 2/41
Brooks, C. J., <u>D.C.M.</u>	1/ 2/41
Willock, G. B. <u>S.</u>, <u>M.M.</u>	1/ 2/41
Hinds, D., <u>D.C.M.</u>	1/ 2/41
Smyth, J.	1/ 2/41
McIntyre, J.	1/ 2/41
McLean, A. D.	1/ 2/41
Button, G. E.	1/ 2/41
Nolan, P.	1/ 2/41
Methven, T.	1/ 2/41

2nd Lieutenants	
Williamson, J.	1/ 2/41
Watson, J. C.	1/ 2/41
Thompson, D. C.	1/ 2/41
Snellie, J.	1/ 2/41
Baxter, M.	1/ 2/41
Battison, J. M., <u>M.M.</u>	1/ 2/41
Cameron, R. F.	1/ 2/41
Little, J. F.	1/ 2/41

2nd Lieutenants - contd.	
Crotch, F. H.	1/ 2/41
McGregor, W.	1/ 2/41
Mackay, K.	1/ 2/41
Rollinson, J. H.	1/ 2/41
Brindle, J.	1/ 2/41

Adjutant & Quarter-Master

Medical-Officer	
Grant, Maj., J. S.,<u>M.B.</u>, F.R.C.S.	1/ 2/41

13th CITY OF GLASGOW (GENERAL
POST OFFICE) BATTALION

Lt.-Colonel	
Teasdale, R.	1/ 2/41

Majors	
Kennedy, J. W. M., (<u>Lt. late H.L.I.</u>)	1/ 2/41
Kilgour, A.	14/ 6/41
Haggart, J. M.	18/ 7/41
Falconer, W. P.	18/ 7/41

Captains	
Montgomery, D.	18/ 7/41
Bennet, D.	18/ 7/41
Stewart, R. J.	19/ 7/41
Robertson, H.	19/ 7/41

Lieutenants	
Robertson, T.	30/ 6/41
Goldie, R.	30/ 6/41
Lang, W.	30/ 6/41
Houston, A.	30/ 6/41
Clerk, J. I.	18/ 7/41
Wilson, F.	18/ 7/41
Blair, J.	18/ 7/41
Storm, J.	18/ 7/41
Sudell,. G. R.	18/ 7/41
Stanage, J.	18/ 7/41

2nd Lieutenants

Adjutant & Quarter-Master

Medical Officer

Commander	Brand, Col. D. E., D.S.O., T.D. (Col. late T.A. Res.) (Hon. Col. T.A.) 1/ 2/41
Signal Officer	Christie, Capt. A. 28/ 6/41
Territorial Army Association administering	County of Lanark T.A. Association, 16 Clydesdale St., Hamilton.

1st LANARKSHIRE BATTALION

Lt.-Colonel

Cranstoun, C. J. E., D.S.O., T.D. (Lt.-Col. ret. T.A.)   1/ 2/41

Majors

Banken, T., T.D. (Maj. late T.A.)   1/ 2/41
McCosh, R., O.B.E., M.C. (Maj. late T.A.)   1/ 2/41
Scott, W. P. (Capt. late T.A.)   1/ 2/41
Fielding, T. H., M.C. (Lt. late T.A.)   1/ 2/41
McLean, W.   1/ 2/41
Provan, D.   1/ 2/41
Howie, K. M. (2/Lt. late T.A.)   1/ 2/41

Captains

Lymington, The Lord, M.C., (Capt. late S. Gds.)   1/ 2/41
Clarkson, A. (Capt. late A.S.C.)   1/ 2/41
McGeachin, W. C. (Capt. late H.L.I.)   1/ 2/41
Brownlee, J. M. (2/Lt. late Rifle Bde.)   1/ 2/41
Wilson, J.   1/ 2/41
Watson, W., D.C.M.   1/ 2/41

Lieutenants

Shersby-Harvie, R. R. (Lt. R.N.V.R.)   1/ 2/41
Johnston, J. W.   1/ 2/41
Donald, C. D., (Capt. late Ind. Army)   1/ 2/41
Hamilton, F. A.   1/ 2/41
Jackson, L.   1/ 2/41
McElroy, J.   1/ 2/41
Russell, R.   1/ 2/41
Taylor, H. J. (Capt. late Gloster R.)   1/ 2/41
Gillespie, A. S. L., (Lt. late Black Watch)   1/ 2/41
Findlater, R., (2/Lt. late H.L.I.)   1/ 2/41
Howe, J. D., M.C.   1/ 2/41

Lieutenants – contd.

Smith, R.   1/ 2/41
Brook, H.   1/ 2/41
Graham, J. B.   1/ 2/41
Wannop, I.   1/ 2/41
Anderson, C. (Lt. late H.L.I.)   1/ 2/41
Brown, D.   1/ 2/41
Watson, P.   1/ 2/41
Baxter, R. P.   1/ 2/41
Hastie, W. F. (Capt. late T.A.)   1/ 2/41
Bayne-Jardine, T. E., D.S.O. (Maj. late R.A.S.C.)   1/ 2/41
Somerville, R.   1/ 2/41

2nd Lieutenants

Draper, C.   1/ 2/41
Rutherford, D. S. (Lt. late Welch R.)   1/ 2/41
Jack, W. W.   1/ 2/41
Megahy, D.   1/ 2/41
Melvin, W.   1/ 2/41
Frame, R., M.M.   1/ 2/41
Smith, A. (Capt. late A. & S.H.)   1/ 2/41
Whitelaw, R.   1/ 2/41
Walker, J., M.M.   1/ 2/41

Adjutant & Quarter-Master

Ross-Taylor, Capt. (actg. 17/3/41) W., R.A.   17/ 3/41

Medical Officers

Adams, Maj. D. V. M., M.B. (Capt. late R.A.M.C.)   1/ 2/41
Petrie, Capt. J., M.B.   1/ 2/41
Thom, Capt., E. G. Y. (Capt. late R.A.M.C.)   14/ 8/41

2nd LANARKSHIRE BATTALION

Lt.-Colonel

Arthur, J. M., C.M.G., D.S.O., (Hon. Col. T.A.)	1/ 2/41

Majors

Milne, T. (Lt. late T.A.)	1/ 2/41
Lamberton, J. R., D.S.O., M.C. (Maj. late H.L.I.)	1/ 2/41
Macfarlane, J., M. C.	1/ 2/41
Davie, T. (Capt. late T.A.)	1/ 2/41
Doughty, W., M.C. (Capt. late T.A.)	1/ 2/41
Kirk, J. A. W.	1/ 2/41
Walker, J.	1/ 2/41

Captains

Bell, R. A.	1/ 2/41
Connell, J. N.	1/ 2/41
Davidson, A., (Lt. late R. Fus.)	1/ 2/41
Ferguson, I. R., M.C. (Capt. late R.T.R.)	1/ 2/41
Mulvey, P. V. (Capt. late Gordons)	1/ 2/41
George, J. M. (Capt. late Seaforths)	1/ 2/41

Lieutenants

Atwell, J. W.	1/ 2/41
Breingan, E. M. (Capt. late T.A.)	1/ 2/41
Faulds, J. B.	1/ 2/41
Glen, J. K. T. (F/Lt. late R.A.F.)	1/ 2/41
Hanson, G. R.	1/ 2/41
Hutton, G. L.	1/ 2/41
McCosh, A. R. (2/Lt. late T.A. Res.)	1/ 2/41
McGee, E., M.C. (Lt. late A. & S.H.)	1/ 2/41
McKnight, J.	1/ 2/41

Lieutenants - contd.

Mitchell, W. K., M.M.	1/ 2/41
Page, J. W. (F/Lt. late R.A.F.)	1/ 2/41
Preston, T. (Lt. late Lan. Fus.)	1/ 2/41
Smillie, W.	1/ 2/41
Napier, I. H.	1/ 2/41
Macdougall, G. F. (Lt. late R. Scots)	10/ 6/41
McLellan, A. J.	10/ 6/41
McLachlan, R., M.M.	19/ 6/41
Graham, J. Y.	23/ 6/41
Yates, I. F., M.M.	26/ 6/41

2nd Lieutenants

	Cameron, P. D., (Lt. late R.T.R.)	1/ 2/41
VC	Carmichael, J.	1/ 2/41
	Farmer, J. M.	1/ 2/41
	Hawthorne, J. (2/Lt. late R. Scots)	1/ 2/41
	Neil, T.	1/ 2/41
	Smith, J. F. (2/Lt. late Rifle Bde.)	1/ 2/41
	Downs, A.	1/ 2/41
	Thomson, G. R.	1/ 2/41
	Reilly, A.	1/ 2/41

Adjutant & Quarter-Master

Medical Officer

Murray, Maj. W. (Lt. late H.L.I.)	1/ 2/41

3rd LANARKSHIRE BATTALION

Lt.-Colonel
Houldsworth, J. F. H. (Capt.
late Gordons)

Majors
Wilson, T. C., M.C. (Capt.
late R.T.R.)   1/ 2/41
McLauchlan, M.   1/ 2/41
Skeil, A. P., D.S.O., M.C.
(Lt. late T.A.)   1/ 2/41
Torrance, J. R. (Capt. late
T.A.)   1/ 2/41

Lieutenants - contd.
Taylor, T.   1/ 2/41
Thomson, G. M.   1/ 2/41
Macgregor, G. E.   1/ 2/41
Johnston, J., D.C.M.   1/ 2/41
Anderson, J.   1/ 2/41
Todd, J. W.   1/ 2/41
McLay, J. E.   1/ 2/41
Macdougall, W.   1/ 2/41
Cain, E.   1/ 2/41
Cruikshanks, T.   1/ 2/41
Gordon, I. C.   1/ 2/41
McKenzie, G. C. (Lt. late
Camerons)   1/ 2/41
O'Neil, J.   1/ 2/41
Woods, A. V., M.M.   1/ 2/41
Faulkner, I. J.   1/ 2/41

Captains
Stirrat, M.   1/ 2/41
Robertson, J. K.   1/ 2/41
Paterson, W., M.M.   1/ 2/41
Sommerville, A.   1/ 2/41
Traynor, J. P., (Lt. late
R. Scots)   1/ 2/41

2nd Lieutenants

Adjutant & Quarter-Master

Lieutenants
Pomphrey, W. R.   1/ 2/41
Davidson, J. D.   1/ 2/41
Russell, R.   1/ 2/41
Wright, W.   1/ 2/41
Wilson, H. MacI.   1/ 2/41
Battison, G.   1/ 2/41
Hunter, G. R. (2/Lt. late
Black Watch)   1/ 2/41
Black, W.   1/ 2/41
Frew, J. H., M.M. (2/Lt.
late R. Scots)   1/ 2/41

Medical Officer
Logan, Maj. D. D., D.S.O., M.D.,
F.R.F.P.S. (Lt.-Col. late
R.A.M.C.)   1/ 2/41

4th LANARKSHIRE BATTALION

Lt.-Colonel
Mather, W., (Bt.-Col. T.A.Res.)
(Hon. Col. T.A.) 1/ 2/41

Majors
Logan, J. G., (Capt. late T.A.) 1/ 2/41
Whitson, E. J., M.C., (Capt. late T.A.) 1/ 2/41
Taylor, J. M., M.C., (Capt. late T.A.) 1/ 2/41
Mackie, J. (Lt. late Camerons) 1/ 2/41
Brooks, G., (Lt. late T.A.) 1/ 2/41

Captains
Butler, J. (Lt. late Cameronians) 2/ 6/41
Ross, A. H. 17/ 6/41

Lieutenants
Frew, G. M., (Capt. late Camerons) 1/ 2/41
Wilson, R. O. S., (Lt. late Black Watch) 1/ 2/41
Scott, A. 1/ 2/41
Watson, T., (Capt. late K.O.S.B.) 1/ 2/41
Hastie, P. D., (2/Lt. late T.A.) 1/ 2/41
Rankin, H. A. 1/ 2/41
Duncan, J. U. 1/ 2/41

Lieutenants — contd.
McKay, W. J., M.C., (Capt. late R.A.) 1/ 2/41
Campbell, D. 1/ 2/41
Cameron, D., (Lt. late R.T.R.) 1/ 2/41
Stephen, A.M., M.C., (Maj. late R.G.A.) 1/ 2/41
Graham, P. H., (Capt. late H.L.I.) 1/ 2/41
Harker, C. S. 1/ 2/41
Clark, R. 1/ 2/41
Frame, W. 1/ 2/41
Wemyss, J. 1/ 2/41
Hamilton, A. 1/ 2/41
Menzies, J. M. 1/ 2/41
Pinkerton, J. C., M.C., (2/Lt. late R.A.) 1/ 2/41
Barnard, T. J. 10/ 6/41
Russell, J. 25/ 6/41
Hislop, W. 25/ 6/41
Blair, W. C. 25/ 6/41

2nd Lieutenant
Bedford, T. F. 1/ 2/41

Adjutant & Quarter-Master

Medical Officer
Thomson, Maj., J. A.
(Capt. late R.A.M.C.) 1/ 2/41

GLASGOW AREA – contd.

NO. 2 ZONE (LANARK) – contd.

5th LANARKSHIRE BATTALION

Lt.-Colonel

Paterson, J. R., (Lt.
late T.A.)   1/ 2/41

Majors

Douglas, W. L., M.C., (Capt.
late R. Scots)   1/ 2/41
Lamont, J. C., (Lt. late
M.G. Corps)   1/ 2/41
Ramage, J. M.M. (Lt. late T.A.)   1/ 2/41
Lever, H. F., D.C.M.   1/ 2/41
Whitton, J.   1/ 2/41
Wotherspoon, A. J. D.   1/ 2/41
Taggart, H. R., (Maj. late T.A)   1/ 2/41

Captains

Murray, A. L. (2/Lt. late R.A)   1/ 2/41
Croll, A. G., (2/Lt. late
Border R.)   1/ 2/41
Gilett, W. J.   1/ 2/41
Scott, R., (2/Lt. late
Seaforth)   1/ 2/41
Mathewson, K. D.   1/ 2/41
Rowbottom, G. H.   1/ 2/41
Harvey, J. G., (Capt. late
H.L.I.   1/ 2/41
Bell, C. K.   31/ 7/41

Lieutenants

Burns, J. A., (Lt. late T.A.)   1/ 2/41
Arbuckle, A., (Lt. late T.A.)   1/ 2/41
Laird, W. C., M.M.   1/ 2/41
Walker, T.   1/ 2/41
Leggate, G.   1/ 2/41
Mackie, A. J.   1/ 2/41
Marson, A.   1/ 2/41
Graham, J. C.   1/ 2/41
Stewart, I. D., (F/Lt. late
R.A.F.)   1/ 2/41
Howat, A.   1/ 2/41
Rogerson, R. B., (Lt. late
T.A.)   1/ 2/41
Rennie, F.   1/ 2/41

5655-3(90)

Lieutenants – contd.

Fordyce, J. H.   1/ 2/41
Hulme, H. G.   1/ 2/41
Docherty, P., D.C.M., M.M.   1/ 2/41
Scott-Maxwell, I. S., (2/Lt.
late T.A. Res.)   1/ 2/41
Currie, J.   1/ 2/41
Miller, J.   1/ 2/41
Hay, G. M.   1/ 2/41
Macintyre, J. (F/O late R.A.F.)   1/ 2/41
Macdougall, A. F.   1/ 2/41
Denny, D. R.   1/ 2/41
Horsburgh, J. R.   1/ 2/41
Lunan, H. J.   1/ 2/41
Connor, J. D. M.   10/ 7/41

2nd Lieutenants

Keane, M. J.   1/ 2/41
Rothwell, J. E., (Lt. late
R.E.)   1/ 2/41
Smith, G. M.   1/ 2/41
Smith, J.   1/ 2/41
Watson, G. M., (Lt. late
A. & S.H.)   1/ 2/41
Lennox, W. (Capt. late
R.A.O.C.)   1/ 2/41
Oliphant, J. B.   1/ 2/41
Kennedy, A.   1/ 2/41
Gogan, J.   1/ 2/41
Frew, J. M., M.C., (Maj.
late Cameronians)   1/ 2/41

Adjutant & Quarter-Master

Medical Officer

Hutchison, Maj. B., M.C.,
(Capt. late R.A.M.C.)   1/ 2/41

6th LANARKSHIRE BATTALION

Lt.-Colonel
MaCrae, W. D., M.C., T.D.,
(Bt.-Col. ret T.A.) 1/ 2/41

Majors
Mundell, J. B., (Maj. late T.A.) 1/ 2/41
Hamilton, R. K., (Capt. late
T.A.) 1/ 2/41
Ross, J. (Lt. late R.A.F.) 1/ 2/41
Henderson, R. R., M.M. 1/ 7/41
Cunningham, J. S. 1/ 7/41

Captains
Gordon, A., (Lt. late
Cameronians) 1/ 2/41
Napier, W. H., (Capt. late R.E.) 1/ 2/41
Ford, J. W. 1/ 2/41

Lieutenants
Peat, G. B. 1/ 2/41
Hilling, A. 1/ 2/41
Anderson, J. 1/ 2/41
Brassington, W. D. (Capt.
late Cameronians) 1/ 2/41
Copeland, J. 1/ 2/41
Hutton, A. N. (Capt. late
A. & S.H.) 1/ 2/41
Melvin, W. S. 1/ 2/41
Couper, A. 1/ 2/41
Ross, J. R., M.M. 1/ 2/41
Masterton, F. D. 1/ 2/41
Smellie, T. T. 1/ 2/41
White, J. L. 1/ 2/41
Young, J. 1/ 7/41
Munro, R. 1/ 7/41

2nd Lieutenants
Bell, W. 1/ 2/41
McIlroy, I. 1/ 2/41
Breingan, J. 1/ 2/41

2nd Lieutenants – contd.
MacMillan, P. G. 1/ 2/41
Kirk, W. 1/ 2/41
Allan, W. R. 1/ 2/41
Macnab, W. 1/ 2/41
Blair, J. H. 1/ 2/41
Goodman, T. 1/ 2/41
Solly, J. W. 1/ 2/41
Fraser, A. 1/ 2/41
Finlayson, T. D. 1/ 2/41
Currie, J. 1/ 2/41
Robb, J. 1/ 2/41
Robson, A. H. 1/ 2/41
Jamieson, N. A. 1/ 2/41
Inglis, R. 1/ 2/41
Brown, T. 1/ 2/41
Armstrong, A. C. 1/ 2/41
Hinshalwood, R. K., (2/Lt.
late R.E.) 1/ 2/41
Tannahill, R. 1/ 2/41
Stewart, A. 1/ 2/41
Downes, J. J. 1/ 2/41
Nicol, R. 1/ 2/41
Cavinue, W. 1/ 2/41
Paterson, W. 1/ 2/41
Clark, N. 1/ 2/41
Logan, J. M. 1/ 2/41
Grady, P. 1/ 2/41
Frame, W. D. 1/ 2/41
Ritchie, W. M. 1/ 2/41
Page, R. E. T. 1/ 7/41
Scott, D. 5/ 8/41
McCallum, J. B. 5/ 8/41

Adjutant & Quarter-Master
Rogerson, Capt. (accg. 2/5/41)
A., Gen. List Inf. 2/ 5/41

Medical Officer
Robertson, Maj. I. C., M.B.,
(Lt. late Ind. Med. Serv.) 1/ 2/41

GLASGOW AREA - contd.

No. 3 ZONE (AYR)

Commander	Dalrymple-Hamilton, Col. N. V. C., C.V.O., (Lt.-Col. Res. of Off.)	1/ 2/41
Second-in-Command	Greenlees, Lt.-Col. W. L., (Maj. late S. Gds.)	1/ 2/41
Chief Guide	Neilson, Maj., J. A. (Maj. late T.A.)	10/ 6/41
Intelligence Officer	Auld, Capt. R., (F/Lt. late R.A.F.)	24/ 6/41
Liaison Officer	Morison, Maj. C. G. T. (Capt. ret.)	21/ 7/4
	Kennedy, Capt., N., D. S. O., T. D. (Bt. Col. late T.A.)	1/ 2/41
Territorial Army Association administering	County of Ayr T.A. Association, 6, Wellington Square, Ayr.	

GROUP NO. 1

Commander	Dunlop, Col. T. C., T.D. (Bt.-Col. ret. T.A.)	1/ 2/4

1st AYRSHIRE BATTALION

Lt.-Colonel

Majors

Crawford, A. R., T.D. (Col. late T.A.)	1/ 2/41
Eglinton & Winton, The Earl of (Maj. late L.G.)	1/ 2/41
Hill, A. H., M.C. (Maj. late T.A.)	1/ 2/41
Nairn, J. M., M.C. (Capt. late T.A.)	1/ 2/41
Laughland, J. T., M.C. (Maj. late T.A.)	1/ 2/41
Hutchison, W. O. (Capt. late R.A.)	1/ 2/41

Captains

Phillips, D. M. P. (Capt. late M.G. Corps)	1/ 2/41
Frew, J. B., M.C. (Lt. late R.S.Fus.)	1/ 2/41
Cameron, W.	1/ 2/41

Lieutenants

Docherty, J. Y.	1/ 2/41
Kerr, J. R., T.D., (Lt.-Col. late T.A.)	1/ 2/41
Scott, C. S. (Capt. late T.A.)	1/ 2/41
Oliphant, A. M. (Lt. late H.L.I.)	1/ 2/41
Donald, J. A. (Capt. late T.A.)	1/ 2/41
Hirst, T. W. (Lt. T.A. Res.)	1/ 2/41
Robertson, J. F.	1/ 2/41

Lieutenants - contd.

Johnston, A. R. (Capt. late R.A.F.)	1/ 2/41
Mackinnon, J.	1/ 2/41
Wilkie, R. C. (Lt. late R. Scots)	1/ 2/41
Laughlan, R. H.	1/ 2/41
Illingworth, A.	1/ 2/41
Breckenridge, J. C.	1/ 2/41
Hopperton, H.	1/ 2/41
Orr, J. M.	1/ 2/41
Cohen, A. M.	22/ 5/41
Howie, A. A.	22/ 5/41

2nd Lieutenants

Hamilton, S.	1/ 2/4
Macdonald, I.	1/ 2/4
Bell, J. H., M.M.	1/ 2/4
Logue, H.	1/ 2/4
Arbuthnott, J. G.	1/ 2/4
Munro, J.	1/ 2/4
Arnott, A.	1/ 2/4
Miller, A. S., M.C. (Lt. late A. & S.H.)	1/ 2/4
Gray, R. S.	1/ 2/4
Forrest, S.	1/ 2/4
Macnamara, D.	1/ 2/4
Mair, J. M.	8/ 8/4
Savage, A. D.	8/ 8/4

Adjutant & Quarter-Master

Medical Officer

Stevenson, Maj. J.	1/ 2/4

2nd AYRSHIRE BATTALION

Lt.-Colonel
Craufurd. Sir Standish, G. G.,
Bt., C.B., C.M.G., C.I.E.,
D.S.O., (Hon. Brig.-Gen. ret.
pay)   1/ 2/41

Majors
Pitcairne-Hill, C. C., (Capt.
late T.A.)   1/ 2/41
Kerr, S.   1/ 2/41
Bell, J. D., (Capt. late R.A.)   1/ 2/41
Cole-Hamilton, J. (F/Lt. late
R.A.F.)   1/ 2/41
Knox-Fletcher, J,   1/ 2/41
Knox, B. (Capt. late R.A.)   10/ 6/41

Captains
Pratt, W. N., (Lt. late
R.S. Fus.)   1/ 2/41
Liptrot, R. (2/Lt. late
R.E.)   1/ 2/41
Anderson, J. A.   1/ 2/41

Lieutenants
Kerr, G. H.   1/ 2/41
Johnston, G. G. H.
(Capt. late R.A.M.C.)   1/ 2/41
Crawford, J. (2/Lt. late
H. G. Corps)   1/ 2/41
Fairley, R. R. (Lt. late
R.A.)   1/ 2/41
Barclay, J., M.M.   1/ 2/41
Cleghorn, J. Y.   1/ 2/41
Gibson, J.   1/ 2/41
McDade, J.   1/ 2/41
McLeish, A. K.   1/ 2/41
McMillan, J. B.   1/ 2/41
Stevenson, H.   1/ 2/41

Lieutenants — contd.
Thomson, T. B. L.   1/ 2/41
Wilson, J.   1/ 2/41
Young, W.   1/ 2/41
Millar, J. N.   1/ 2/41
Neilson, H. R.   20/ 7/41

2nd Lieutenants
Struthers, J. R.   1/ 2/41
McKee, D.   1/ 2/41
Baxter, W.   1/ 2/41
Cashmore, J. McD., M.M.   1/ 2/41
Johnston, J.   1/ 2/41
Forsyth, D. L. P.   1/ 2/41
Brown, D. R.   1/ 2/41
Rush, W. P.   23/ 6/41
Robertson, C. P.   30/ 6/41 .
Beare, B. C.   1/ 7/41
Gardiner, J.   8/ 7/41
Douglas, W.   18/ 7/41
Ramage, J.   21/ 7/41

Adjutant & Quarter-Master
Wilson, Capt. (actg. 1/2/41)
R., Gen. List Inf.   1/ 2/41

Medical Officer
Gordon, Maj. J. S., M.B.   1/ 2/41

137

3rd AYRSHIRE BATTALION

Lt.-Colonel
Walker, J. W., C.M.G., D.S.O.,
T.D. (Hon.-Brig. ret. T.A.)   1/ 2/41

Majors
Breckenridge, M. W., (Maj.
late T.A.)   1/ 2/41
Linton, R. (Maj. late K.R.R.C.) 1/ 2/41
Mackenzie, D. M., M.C., T.D.
(Bt. Maj. late T.A.)   1/ 2/41
Millar, G. L., M.C., (Maj.
late M.G. Corps.)   1/ 2/41

Captains
Currie, J. (Lt. late Ind. Army) 1/ 2/41
Martin, D. M., (F/Lt. late
R.F.C.)   1/ 2/41
Nairn, J. (Lt. late H.L.I.)   1/ 2/41
Thorburn, D. H., (Maj. late
Cameronians)   1/ 2/41

Lieutenants
Scott, R. W.   1/ 2/41
Bicker, D.   1/ 2/41
Agnew, J. P.   1/ 2/41
McKelvie, H. G. (Lt. late
R.S. Fus.)   1/ 2/41
Robertson, R.   1/ 2/41
Nairn, T. K.   1/ 2/41
Steven, J. M.   1/ 2/41
Watson, W. C. (Capt. late
Scottish, Rif.)   1/ 2/41
Cowan, D. M.   1/ 2/41
Harvie, A. W., M.C. (Capt.
late K.O.S.B.)   1/ 2/41
McHoull, D., (Lt. late R.S.
Fus.)   1/ 2/41
Orion, L. C.   1/ 2/41
Boyle, C. R.   1/ 2/41

Lieutenants - contd.
Knox, G. K.   1/ 2/41
McAndrew, Sir Charles G. Knt.
T.D., M.P., (Bt. Col. T.A.
Res.)   1/ 2/41
Brown, A. M.   1/ 2/41
Farmer, E. H. G., D.C.M.   31/ 5/41
McLaughlan, P. J.   31/ 5/41
Dunlop, A.   31/ 5/41
Borland, J. F.   5/ 6/41
Stevenson, R. (Lt. late
A. & S.H.)   13/ 6/41
Allan, A. R. (Lt. late
A. & S.H.)   13/ 6/41
Jenkins, J. L. C., M.C.
(Capt. late Camerons)   13/ 6/41
Easdale, R. N. (Capt. late
H.L.I.)   13/ 6/41
Thomson, T.   16/ 6/41
Howie, J. R.   5/ 7/41

2nd Lieutenants
Goldie, T. (2/Lt. late R.F.A.) 1/ 2/41
Sloan, D. C. R.   1/ 2/41
Mackenzie, A. I. (Lt. late
Lovat Scouts)   1/ 2/41
Gilfillar, H. M.   1/ 2/41
Russell, A. R. (Capt. late
R.A.F.)   1/ 2/41
Barclay, T.   1/ 2/41

Adjutant & Quarter-Master
Frew, Capt. (actg. 17/4/41) A.,
Gen. List Inf.   17/ 4/41

Medical Officer
McCulloch, Maj. A. W., M.B.,
(2/Lt. late R.A.F.)   1/ 2/41

GLASGOW AREA — contd.

NO.3 ZONE (AYR) — contd.

GROUP NO.1 — contd.

4th AYRSHIRE BATTALION

Lt.-Colonel
Wilkie, D. M., T.D., (Lt.-Col.
ret. T.A.)   1 / 2/41

Majors
Farrar, H. B.   1 / 2/41
Paton, E. R. (Lt. late T.A.)   1 / 2/41
Tulloch, R.   1 / 2/41
Morton, R. (Capt. late R.A.)   1 / 2/41
Jamieson, K. (Lt. late R.A.F.) 1 / 2/41
Brodie, W. A. (Capt. late
T.A.)   1 / 2/41

Captains
Keddie, J., D.C.M.   1 / 2/41
Ferguson, T. (2/Lt. late
H.L.I.)   1 / 2/41
Brown, W. C.   1 / 2/41
Reid, R. W. T. (Lt. late
M.G. Corps)   1 / 2/41
Bell, A. R. (2/Lt. late
R.S. Fus.)   1 / 2/41

Lieutenants
White, C. A.   1 / 2/41
Ewing, W.   1 / 2/41
Carruthers, D. (Capt. late
R.S. Fus.)   1 / 2/41
Brown, J. R., D.C.M.   1 / 2/41
Shaw, E. W. (Lt. late R.A.F.) 1/ 2/41
Dick, M.   1 / 2/41
Bunce, A.   1 / 2/41
Laing, H. H.   1 / 2/41
Scott, J. (Lt. late T.A.)   1 / 2/41
Smith, C. V.   1 / 2/41

Lieutenants — contd.
Ritchie, J. S.   1 / 2/41
Clark, G.   1 / 2/41
Crowder, C. W.   1 / 2/41
Wardhaugh, D.   1 / 2/41
Morton, T.   1 / 2/41
Gebbie, J. L.   1 / 2/41
Mackie, J. W.   1 / 2/41
Archie, W. M., (2/Lt. late
A. & S.H.)   1 / 2/41
Mackeggie, G. A.   1 / 2/41
Clibbon, D. S.   1 / 2/41
Morrison, P., M.C., (Lt. late
A. & S.H.)   1 / 2/41
Robertson, W. A.   30/ 6/41
McCrae, A. T.   9/ 7/41
Macfarlane, M.   24/ 7/41

2nd Lieutenants
Edgar, R.   1 / 2/41
Stevenson, J. L.   1 / 2/41
Brown, A.   1 / 2/41
Dempster, W. H.   1 / 2/41
Gilchrist, R. A.   1 / 2/41
Cunnison, J. B.   1 / 2/41
Anderson, W.   1 / 2/41
Swallow, F. J.   1 / 2/41
West, H. C.   1 / 2/41
McKay, W.   1 / 2/41
Kearney, P.   1 / 2/41
Hamilton, T. L.   1 / 2/41
Goudie, R. W.   1 / 2/41
Wilson, J.   18/ 6/41

Adjutant & Quarter-Master
-

Medical Officer
Robertson, Maj. A. (Lt. late
R.S. Fus.)   1 / 2/41

56455-3(95)

159

GLASGOW AREA - ;contd.
NO. 3 ZONE (AYR) - contd.
GROUP NO. 1 - contd.

5TH AYRSHIRE BATTALION		6TH AYRSHIRE BATTALION	
Lt.-Colonel		Lt.-Colonel	
Arthur, E. S.,		Cross, A. R., M.C., T.D.	
(Lt. late The Greys)	1/ 2/41	(Lt.-Col. T.A. Res.)	1/ 2/41
Majors		Majors	
Laidlaw, R. (Lt. late The		Inglis, J. J. (Maj. late	
Greys)	1/ 2/11	Ind. Army)	1/ 2/41
Ross, D. (Capt. late A.V.C.)	1/ 2/41	Montgomerie, J. C.	1/ 2/41
Leitch, R..McH.	1/ 2/41	Dubes, C. I. A., T.D.	
Taylor. T.,.T. (Lt. late		(Lt.-Col. late T.A.)	1/ 2/41
R.A.F.)	1/ 2/41	Merson, A. J. (Capt. late	
Paterson,. R. C.		R.S. Fus.)	1/ 2/41
(Capt. late T.A.)	1/ 2/41		
		Captains	
Captains		Turnbull, J. C. (Capt.	
Park, J., M.M.	1/ 2/41	late H.L.I.)	1/ 2/41
Hogg, J. R. (2/Lt. late		McKellar, W. T. (Lt. late T.A.)	1/ 2/41
R.A.F.)	1/ 2/41	Lamington, Lord	
Kippen, A. C.	1/ 2/41	M.C. (Capt. late S. Gds.)	1/ 2/41
Crawford, A. T. (Capt.			
late T.A.)	1/ 2/41	Lieutenants	
		Maclehose, H. A., (Maj. late	
Lieutenants		Sco. Rif.)	1/ 2/41
Parker, A.	1/ 2/41	Wilson, J., M.M.	1/ 2/41
Findlay, T.	1/ 2/41	Harvey, J. (Capt. late Hussars)	1/ 2/41
Penman, A.	1/ 2/41	Auld, T., D.C.M., M.M.	1/ 2/41
Matthews, S. C.	1/ 2/41	Boyle, A., D.C.M.	1/ 2/41
Bain, M.	1/ 2/41	Kellighan, G. B.	1/ 2/41
Truggan, A. S.	1/ 2/41	Paterson, J. M.	1/ 2/41
Macdonald, A. A.	1/ 2/41	Gillespie, J.	1/ 2/41
Stobbs, T.	1/ 2/41	Hunter, J. R.	1/ 2/41
Bell, W.	1/ 2/41	Winter, D. (Capt. late W.I.R.)	1/ 2/41
Bryson, A. (2/Lt. late		McIntosh, D. L.	1/ 2/41
R.S. Fus.)	1/ 2/41	Mitchell, A. C. (2/Lt. late	
Whyte, R. S.	1/ 2/41	Camerons)	26/ 5/41
Smith, W.	1/ 2/41	Parker, W. C.	28/ 5/41
Balsillie, C.	1/ 2/41		
Ho d, J.	22/ 5/41		
2nd Lieutenants		2nd Lieutenants	
Tanner, T. S.	1/ 2/41	Macpherson, J. D.	1/ 2/41
Geekie, D. G., D.C.M.	1/ 2/41	McAthster, J.	1/ 2/41
Watson, W. M.	1/ 2/41		
Goudie, W.	1/ 2/41		
Morrison, R.	1/ 2/41	Adjutant & Quarter-Master	
Hamilton, D. B.	1/ 2/41	Malins, Capt., (actg. 1/2/41)	
Shankly, J.	1/ 2/41	E. F. J. (R.A.(T.A.))	1/ 2/41
Ewing, A. J.	1/ 2/41		
Scoular, J. C.	1/ 2/41		
Adjutant & Quarter-Master			
Medical Officer		Medical Officer	
Campbell, Maj. A. M. M.B.	7/ 7/41	Walker, Maj. R. M., M.D.	
		(Capt. late R.A.M.C.)	1/ 2/41

7TH AYRSHIRE (AYR) BATTALION

Lt.-Colonel
MacBrayne, P. J., M.C.
(Maj. ret. Ind. Army)   1/ 2/41

Majors
Gardiner, P. P. L., M.C.
(Capt. late A. & S.H.)   1/ 2/41
Lanham, W. S.   1/ 2/41
Parker, I. T., M.C.
(Capt. late R.S. Fus.)   1/ 2/41
Kennedy, A. S.   1/ 2/41
Fulton, A. J., M.M.   1/ 2/41
Mackenzie, A. (Capt. late
R.A.F.)   1/ 2/41
Leitch, H. (Capt. late
Camerons)   1/ 2/41

Captains
Stevenson, J., M.C. (2/Lt.
late Rifle Bde.)   1/ 2/41
McDonald, D. S. H.   1/ 2/41
Kinghorn, J. A.   1/ 2/41
McGregor, D.   1/ 2/41
Bond, W.   1/ 2/41
Paton, A.   1/ 2/41

Lieutenants
Stewart, C. I.   1/ 2/41
Ady, C. J.   1/ 2/41
Fowler, J. J. (2/Lt. late
Gordons)   1/ 2/41
Macrae, R. M. (Lt. late
A. & S.H.)   1/ 2/41
McInstray, T. D.   1/ 2/41
Kelso, R. L.   1/ 2/41
Kennie, D. W. (Capt. late
Ind. Army)   1/ 2/41
Smith, M. S. (2/Lt. late
R.S. Fus.)   1/ 2/41
Laing, G.   1/ 2/41
Wilson, J. M., M.M.   1/ 2/41
Matthews, W. G.   1/ 2/41
Fairbairn, G. (Lt. late
R.S. Fus.)   1/ 2/41
Bell, R. A.   1/ 2/41
Kirkman, G.   1/ 2/41
Maitland, A.   1/ 2/41
Cameron, M. C.   1/ 2/41
Stewart, A. H.   1/ 2/41
Alcorn, J.   1/ 2/41
Topping, J. L.   1/ 2/41
Wilkinson, W. A.   1/ 2/41
Hopkin, F. W.   1/ 2/41

Lieutenants – contd.
Macgregor, J.   1/ 2/41
Murray, R. C.   1/ 2/41
Lapham, T. H.   1/ 2/41
Kilgour, J. M.   1/ 2/41
Anderson, G. (Lt. late R.A.)   7/ 7/41
Tweedie, H. T.   7/ 7/41
Graves E. (Capt. late
Ind. Army)   1/ 8/41

2nd Lieutenants
Mitchell, W. (Lt. late
R.S. Fus.)   1/ 2/41
Miller, J.   1/ 2/41
Robertson, T. A. G.   1/ 2/41
Fidler, W. T.   1/ 2/41
Paterson, J. A.   1/ 2/41
Wright, N. C. (2/Lt. late
R. Berks R.)   1/ 2/41
McCallum, J. C.   1/ 2/41
Haining, P.   1/ 2/41
McCormack, W.   1/ 2/41
Thomson, C. M.   1/ 2/41
Mackie, W. G.   1/ 2/41
Paterson, J. A.   1/ 2/41
Ritchie, W. S. (Capt. late
A. & S.H.)   1/ 2/41
Cunningham, A. (Capt.
late R.A.S.C.)   1/ 2/41
Leitch, H. (Capt. late
Camerons)   1/ 2/41
Blane, W.   1/ 2/41
Waddell, T., D.C.M.   1/ 2/41
Coutts, K.   1/ 2/41
Boyd, J. G.   1/ 2/41
Bell, S. J.   1/ 2/41
Smith, O.   1/ 2/41
Gibson, J.   1/ 2/41
Craig, R.   1/ 2/41

Adjutant & Quarter-Master

Medical Officer
Bennatyne, Maj., B. M. P.   1/ 2/41

GLASGOW AREA - contd.

NO. 3 ZONE (AYR) - contd.

GROUP No. 1 - contd.

8th AYRSHIRE (ARDEER) BATTALION

Lt.-Colonel
Gale, L., M.C. (Maj. late E.
York R.)   1/ 2/41

Majors
Craik, J. (Capt. late T.A.)   1/ 2/41
Macaulay, R. W. (Capt. late
T.A.)   1/ 2/41
Morgan, R., M.M.   1/ 2/41
Baldock, P. A.   1/ 2/41
Marke, D. J. B.(Lt. late
R.A.O.C.)   1/ 2/41

Captains
Burns, R.   1/ 2/41
Traill, D.   1/ 2/41
Rae, G. (Lt. late R.
War. R.)   1/ 2/41
Birrell, J. (Lt. late
R.A.)   1/ 2/41
Campbell, P. M. (Capt. T.A.)   1/ 2/41

Lieutenants
Hamilton, T. C. (Lt. late
T.A.)   1/ 2/41
Bensted, H. C.   1/ 2/41
Craik, G. L. (Capt. late
H.L.I.)   1/ 2/41
Muir, J. C.   1/ 2/41
Morris, G.   1/ 2/41
Houghton, A. A.   1/ 2/41
Levesley, A. S.   1/ 2/41
Evans, S. G.   1/ 2/41
Macfarlane, J.   1/ 2/41
McLaughlan, R. T. (Lt. late
E. York R.)   1/ 2/41
Local, J., M.C. (Lt. late
E. York R.)   1/ 2/41
Hornet, J. C.   1/ 2/41
Huck, S.   1/x2/41

2nd Lieutenants
Shaw, R. W.   1/ 2/41
Fawcett, J. D.   1/ 2/41
Tolmie, A. C.   1/ 2/41

Adjutant & Quarter-Master

Medical Officer
Daly, Maj. J.   1/ 2/41

SOUTH CARRICK COMPANY

Lt.-Colonel

Major
Fleming, J. K. S., C.B.E. (Lt.-
Col. late Ind. Med. Serv.)   1/ 2/41

Captains

Lieutenants
Hewetson, H. J.   1/ 2/41
Dunsmuir, G. A.   1/ 2/41
Gray, D. I. W. (Lt. T.A. Res.)   1/ 2/41

2nd Lieutenants
Arid, W. F.   1/ 2/41

Adjutant & Quarter-Master

Medical Officer
Kitchin, Maj. A. S., M.B.,   1/ 2/41

GLASGOW AREA - contd.

No. 4 ZONE (DUMBARTON)

Commander	Speirs, Col. G. C. T. M.C., T.D. (Col. T.A.) 1/ 2/41
Zone Liaison Officer	Carswell, Lt. H. G., M.C. (Capt. late Sco. Rif.) 1/ 2/41
Territorial Army Association administering	Dumbarton T.A. Association, Benhill Road, Dumbarton.

1st DUMBARTON BATTALION

Lt.-Colonel
Findlay, T. D., (Maj. ret. T.A.) 1/ 2/41

Majors
Caldwell, T. C. (Capt. late Suppy. Res.) 1/ 2/41
Thomson, A. G. (Lt. late R.A.F.) 1/ 2/41
Topping, F. R. (Lt.-Col. late R.A.S.C.) 1/ 2/41
Hunt, R. T. (Capt. late E. Lan. R.)

Captains
Hosie, J., M.B.E. 1/ 2/41
Cotton, E. W. (Capt. late R.E.) 1/ 2/41
MacLachlan, W. K., D.S.O. (Maj. late R. North'd Fus.) 1/ 2/41

Lieutenants
Pickup, H. 1/ 2/41
Houston, J. L. 1/ 2/41
Watkinson, E. 1/ 2/41
Brown, J. 1/ 2/41
McDonald, J. (Capt. late T.A.)1/ 2/41
Bryce, G. H. 1/ 2/41
Barrie, R. W. 1/ 2/41
Ord, J. W. 1/ 2/41
Marshall, W. D. K. 1/ 2/41
Gibson, J. H. (2/Lt. late R.A.F.) 1/ 2/41
Duncan, A., M.C.

Lieutenants - contd.
Millar, A. S. (Capt. late A. & S.H.) 1/ 2/41
Murdoch, J. D., M.C., T.D. (Lt.-Col. late T.A.) 1/ 2/41
Blundell, R. W. (2/Lt. late R. Mar.) 1/ 2/41
Morison, J. H. 1/ 2/41
Fairburn, G., M.C. (Capt. late R.E.) 1/ 2/41
Figg, J. H. (Capt. late T.A.) 1/ 2/41
Russell, T. R. (Lt. late T.A.) 1/ 2/41
Harrison, I. R. (Lt.-Col. late R.A.) 1/ 2/41
McAndrew, A. (Capt. late Ind. Army) 26/ 6/41
Fuller, T. W. (Capt. late York H.) 26/ 6/41
Snodgrass, E. I. (Capt. late R. Signals) 16/ 7/41

2nd Lieutenants
Mitchell, A. 1/ 2/41
McAulay, J. R. 1/ 2/41
Cunningham, J. 1/ 2/41
Blaikie, F. W. L. 1/ 2/41
Lawther, W. (Lt. late R. Scots) 1/ 2/41
Campbell, J. (2/Lt. late R.A.F.) 1/ 2/41
Gray, A. A. (2/Lt. late R.A.) 1/ 2/41
McGruer, J. 1/ 2/41
Smellie, W. R. (Lt. late R.A.) 1/ 2/41
Paton, H. E. J. (Lt. late R.A.) 1/ 2/41
Birkmere, J. 14/ 8/41
Charleson, C. M. 20/ 8/41

Adjutant & Quarter-Master
Scrimgeour, Capt. (actg. 11/2/41) D. Gen. List Inf. 21/ 2/41

Medical Officer
Findlay, Maj. T. C., M.B. 1/ 2/41

56455-3(99)

2nd DUMBARTON BATTALION

Lt.-Colonel
MacCarrell, A. L., D.S.O., T.D.,
(Maj. ret. T.A.)   1/ 2/41

Majors
Riddell, N. C. (Maj. late
R.A.F.)   1/ 2/41
Green, J. (2/Lt. late A. &
S.H.)   1/ 2/41
McNeill, J. M., M.C. (Maj.
late R.F.A.)   1/ 2/41
Graham, D. T.   1/ 2/41
Tideman, C. G.   1/ 2/41

Captains
Johnston, J. H. (Capt. late
Rifle Bde.)   1/ 2/41
Ballantyne, A. R.   1/ 2/41
Heron, J.   1/ 2/41
Milne, G. G. (Lt. late
London Scottish)   24/ 7/41

Lieutenants
Shields, P.   1/ 2/41
Fleming, J. G. (Lt. late
A. & S.H.)   1/ 2/41
Carwardine, W.   1/ 2/41
Gibson, J. R.   1/ 2/41
Beattie, R. A.   1/ 2/41
Baillie, G. G.   1/ 2/41
Taylor, J. S. (Lt. late
R. North'd Fus.)   1/ 2/41
McLeish, W. J.   1/ 2/41
Teitge, C.   1/ 2/41
Thomson, J. H.   1/ 2/41
Borthwick, J.   1/ 2/41

56455-3(100)

Lieutenants - contd.
Donaldson, W.   1/ 2/41
Boyd, W.   1/ 2/41
MacIntyre, J. B.   1/ 2/41
Hughes, A.   1/ 2/41
Wharton, J., M.C. (Capt.
late R.A.S.C.)   1/ 2/41
Sinclair, J. I.   1/ 2/41
Murdoch, H. P.   8/ 7/41
Dalgleish, T. D.   8/ 7/41
Bex, C.   8/ 7/41
Inch, J., D.C.M.   8/ 7/41
Fisher, D. T.   8/ 7/41
Scott, C. M.   8/ 7/41
Macintyre, T.   18/ 7/41

2nd Lieutenants
Brown, J.   1/ 2/41
McGrath, R., M.M.   1/ 2/41
Thomson, T.   1/ 2/41
Wilson, T. S.   1/ 2/41
Parker, W. H. D.   1/ 2/41
Davies, J. H.   8/ 7/41
Dawson, J. P.   8/ 7/41
Munro, N.   8/ 7/41
Taylor, D.   18/ 7/41
Scott, A.   18/ 7/41
Orrock, A. A.   12/ 8/41

Adjutant & Quarter-Master

Medical Officer
Meiland, Maj. N., M.B.,   1/ 2/41

3rd DUMBARTON BATTALION

Lt.-Colonel
Hepburn, P. B., M.C. (Capt. late T.A.)   1/ 2/41

Majors
Park, J. B., M.C. (Capt. late Camerons)   1/ 2/41
Rodger, A. G. B., M.M.   1/ 2/41
Alexander, W. S. (Capt. late T.A.)   1/ 2/41
Ferguson, H., M.C. (Lt. late R.E.)   1/ 2/41

Captains
Ronald, A. W. (2/Lt. late H.L.I.)   1/ 2/41
Sutherland, J. A. H. (Capt. late Cameronians)   1/ 2/41
Thomson, P.   1/ 2/41
McLaren, J. G., M.M.   1/ 2/41
Logan, J. (Capt. late R. Scots)   8/ 8/41

Lieutenants
Russell, H. M. (Capt late H.L.I.)   1/ 2/41
White, R. K. V. (Capt. late R. North'd. Fus.)   1/ 2/41
Dears, A. G.   1/ 2/41
Frame, A. (Capt. late A. & S.H.)   1/ 2/41
Low, J. M. (2/Lt. late R. Scots)   1/ 2/41
McLaughlin, B. (2/Lt. late Worc. R.)   1/ 2/41
Ballingall, A. M., M.C., V.D. (Late R. Scots.)   1/ 2/41
Pogson, W.   . 1/ 2/41
Learmouth, J. S.   1/ 2/41
Bark, E.   1/ 2/41
Dunsmore, T. S.   1/ 2/41
Mitchell, J.   1/ 2/41
Crawford, A. (Lt. late R. Scots)   1/ 2/41
Hill, C.   1/ 2/41

Lieutenants – contd.
Broadhead, E. (Lt. late M.G. Corps)   1/ 2/41
McCarroll, J.   1/ 2/41
McCash, J.   1/ 2/41
Whyte, R.   1/ 2/41
Tod, A. H.   1/ 2/41
Nicholson, A. H.   1/ 2/41
Dunlop, W.   1/ 2/41
Maguire, R., M.C., (Capt. late R. Dub. Fus.)   1/ 2/41
Brodie, P. P.   1/ 2/41

2nd Lieutenants
McDowell, D. (Lt. late Black Watch)   1/ 2/41
Ferguson, H. (Lt. late A. & S.H.)   1/ 2/41
Jackson, W.   1/ 2/41
Maccowan, J.   1/ 2/41
Kennedy, R. H. M.   1/ 2/41
Thomson, A. M.   1/ 2/41
Macdonald, A. (Maj. late T.A.)   1/ 2/41
Scott, R. P. T. (Lt. late D.C.L.I.)   1/ 2/41
Anderson, H. S. (Lt. late R.F.A.)   1/ 2/41
Forster, R. A. (Capt. late R. North'd. Fus.)   1/ 2/41
Houstoun, S. E.   1/ 2/41
Walmsley, D. C., M.M.   1/ 2/41
Jamieson, J. A.   1/ 2/41
Williamson, R. M.   7/ 7/41
Taig, A.   7/ 7/41
Stark, J.   7/ 7/41
Cameron, T. P.   7/ 7/41

Adjutant & Quarter-Master

Medical Officer
Pirie, Maj., G. J., M.B.   1/ 2/41

GLASGOW AREA - contd.

NO.5 ZONE (RENFREW & BUTE)

Commander	Walker, Col., H. C., T.D., (Bt.-Col. ret. T.A.)	1/ 2/41
Second-in-Command	Walker, Lt.-Col. W. N., M.C., (Capt. late T.A.)	1/ 2/41
Territorial Army Association administering	County of Renfrew T.A. Association, 50, Moss Street, Paisley.	

1st RENFREWSHIRE & BUTESHIRE BATTALION

Lt.-Colonel

Herbert, R. B. (Capt. late Serv. Bn. H.L.I.) 1/ 2/41

Majors

Hill, M. H. L. (Lt.-Col. late T.A.) 1/ 2/41
Mitchell, D. (F/Lt. late R.A.F.) 1/ 2/41
Reid, A. W. (2/Lt. late Black Watch) 1/ 2/41
Morrison, F. (Capt. late A. & S.H.) 1/ 2/41
Gray, W. F. M. (Maj. late T.A.) 1/ 2/41
Hewison, H. M., O.B.E., M.C., T.D., (Bt.-Col. late T.A.) 1/ 2/41
Brown-Fullarton, W. M. (2/Lt. late M.G. Corps) 1/ 2/41
Henderson, J. D. (2/Lt. late T.A.) 1/ 2/41
Hicks, G., M.C., T.D., (Maj. late T.A.) 1/ 2/41
Denholm, W. L. (Lt.-Col. late R.A.) 1/ 2/41

Captains

Macrobert, H. (Capt. late H.L.I.) 1/ 2/41
Brodie, A. A. L. (Capt. late R.A.) 1/ 2/41

Captains - contd.

Holmes, S. A. 1/ 2/41
Rae, A. C. 1/ 2/41
Birkmyre, J. (Capt. late T.A.) 1/ 2/41
Steel, J. H. 1/ 2/41
Watson, C. D. (Capt. late K.O.S.B.) 1/ 2/41
Davie, C. L. B., D.C.M. (Capt. late T.A.) 1/ 2/41
Mackinnon, S. C. (Capt. late Camerons) 1/ 2/41
Templeton, D. 24/ 7/41
McSwein, D. 28/ 7/41

Lieutenants

Scott, A. W. 1/ 2/41
Richardson, J. 1/ 2/41
Allin, G. W. 1/ 2/41
Shearer, J. C. B. (Lt. late R.T.R.) 1/ 2/41
Hardie, W. 1/ 2/41
Gilmour, T. 1/ 2/41
Young, C. F. (Lt. late R.S. Fus.) 1/ 2/41
Skilling, A. 1/ 2/41
Williamson, P. J. F. 1/ 2/41
Morris, J. 1/ 2/41
McTaggart, W. 1/ 2/41
Quiros-Worledge, F. 1/ 2/41
Harkess, J. 1/ 2/41
Trann, J. 1/ 2/41
Crawford, R. A. 1/ 2/41
Clark, J. 1/ 2/41
Miller, W. 1/ 2/41

GLASGOW AREA — contd.

No.5 ZONE (RENFREW & BUTE) — contd.

1st Renfrewshire & Buteshire
Battalion - contd.

Lieutenants — contd.

Darling, E.	1/ 2/41
Charters, F. A.	1/ 2/41
McKillop, D.	1/ 2/41
Duncan, J.	1/ 2/41
Crawford, J.	1/ 2/41
Harvey, F. (2/Lt. late Cameronians)	1/ 2/41
Murray, T. S.	1/ 2/41
Napier, R. G. (Lt. late T.A.)	1/ 2/41
Martin, J. (Capt. late T.A.)	1/ 2/41
Mackenzie, T. G., M.C., T.D. (Maj. late K.O.Y.L.I.)	1/ 2/41
Hedderwick, C. (Lt. late R.E.)	1/ 2/41
Brown, A. (Capt. late K.O.S.B.)	1/ 2/41
Carson, D. S., O.B.E. (Lt.-Col. late Cameronians)	1/ 2/41
Sladden, R. J., M.B.E., D.C.M., (Capt. late R.A.F.)	26/ 6/41
Henderson, W. N.	28/ 7/41

2nd Lieutenants

Murray, J. I. (Lt. late Ind. Army)	1/ 2/41
Caldwell, A. F. (Paymr. Lt. late R.N.R.)	1/ 2/41
Lawrie, D. S.	1/ 2/41
McBride, J. M.	1/ 2/41
Brown, G. W.	1/ 2/41
Mackay, D. B.	1/ 2/41
Lochhead, E. H.	1/ 2/41
Buchanan, J.	1/ 2/41
Swan, J. J.	1/ 2/41
Soutar, A.	1/ 2/41
McAllister, M.	1/ 2/41
Keiller, R. D.	1/ 2/41
Collie Sturrock, N.	1/ 2/41
Anderson, K. H. J. (late W. Somerset Yeo.)	1/ 2/41
Loudon, T.	1/ 2/41
Stirling, J.	1/ 2/41
Edwards, C. F. (Capt. late R.A.)	1/ 2/41

56455-3(103)

2nd Lieutenants — contd.

Brown, W.	1/ 2/41
Butler, H. A.	1/ 2/41
Whytock, J. (Lt. late T.A.)	1/ 2/41
Armit, W. (Lt. late R.A.F.)	1/ 2/41
McGeachie, J. M.	1/ 2/41
Mackay, A. (Lt. late R. Scots)	1/ 2/41
Duncan, R. G.	1/ 2/41
Waddell, W.	1/ 2/41
Ballantyne, J. R. (Capt. late R.E.)	1/ 2/41
Macfarlane, W. F.	1/ 2/41
McCallum, A. S.	1/ 2/41
Leitch, P. A.	1/ 2/41
Matheson, J. M.	1/ 2/41
Miller, C. McD.	1/ 2/41
McKirdy, D. S. L.	19/ 6/41
McKenzie, D.	19/ 6/41
Andrews, W.	19/ 6/41
Hydes, T.	19/ 6/41
Blair, J. E.	19/ 6/41
Martin, W.	19/ 6/41
Foote, W.	19/ 6/41
McLean, R.	19/ 6/41
Brown, J.	19/ 6/41
Hardie, J. B.	12/ 7/41
Kennedy, A.	12/ 7/41

Adjutant & Quarter-Master

Medical Officer

Russell, Maj. J. N., M.B., (Maj. late R.A.M.C.)	1/ 2/41

GLASGOW AREA - contd.

NO.5 ZONE (RENFREW & BUTE) - contd.

2nd RENFREWSHIRE BATTALION

Lt.-Colonel
Macrobert, J. (Capt. late
T.A.)   1/ 2/41

Majors
Barclay, R. C. (Capt. late
A. & S.H.)   1/ 2/41
Gardner, J. (Capt. late
A. & S.H.)   1/ 2/41
Campbell, J. C., T.D. (Lt.-Col.
late T.A.)   1/ 2/41
Ballantyne, G. B. (Capt. late
M.G. Corps)   1/ 2/41
Branker, J.   1/ 2/41
Lang, W. D. (Lt. late
A. & S.H.)   1/ 2/41
Greenlees, R. C. (Lt. late
A. & S.H.)   1/ 2/41
Picken, J.   1/ 2/41
Simpson, J.   1/ 2/41
Morrison, J. E., M.C. (Lt.
late M.G. Corps)   1/ 2/41

Captains
Walton, T. H.   1/ 2/41
Henry, S. J. (Lt. late R.
Scots)   1/ 2/41
Gibson, N. J. (Lt. late Lan.
Fus.)   1/ 2/41
Baird, A. (Lt. late R.A.F.)   1/ 2/41
Semple, G. J.   1/ 2/41

Captains - contd.
Corson McClelland, W. (Capt.
late A. & S.H.)   1/ 2/41
Jack, J. S. M. (Capt. late
T.A.)   1/ 2/41

Lieutenants
Gardiner, H. McL. (Late Res. of
Off.)   1/ 2/41
Murray, A. T. K.   1/ 2/41
McGee, D. McL. (2Lt. late
T.A.)   1/ 2/41
Souden, S. (Lt. late
H.L.I.)   1/ 2/41
Whitson, F.   1/ 2/41
Caldwell, K. L.   1/ 2/41
Walker, W. F. (Lt. late
A. & S.H.)   1/ 2/41
Craig, A.   1/ 2/41
Emsley, D.   1/ 2/41
Campbell, J.   1/ 2/41
Gourlay, J. McK.   1/ 2/41
Gregg, C. J.   1/ 2/41
Barr, H. C.   1/ 2/41
Semple, J. C.   1/ 2/41
Stirling, W. T., D.C.M.   1/ 2/41
Bradley, R. A.   1/ 2/41
Alexander, R. D.   1/ 2/41
Buchanan, J. (Lt. late
Black Watch)   1/ 2/41
Begg, D. H. (Capt. late
T.A.)   1/ 2/41
Donaldson, F. A.   1/ 2/41
Coats, G. S.   1/ 2/41
Lee, J.   1/ 2/41
Johnstone, J. H., T.D.
(Maj. late R.S. Fus.)   1/ 2/41
Gow, L. H. (Capt. late T.A.
Res.)   1/ 2/41
Nicholl, J. M. (Capt. late
T.A.)   1/ 2/41
Peck, C. E. (Lt. S. Lan. R.)   1/ 2/41
Scott, C. A., M.C. (Capt.
late S. Stafford R.)   1/ 2/41

2nd Renfrewshire & Buteshire Battalion
— contd.

Lieutenants — contd.

Anderson, T. B.	1/ 2/41
Reid, J. (Capt. late	
K.O.Y.L.I.)	1/ 2/41
Love, J. B. (Lt. late H.L.I.)	1/ 2/41
Wilson, F.	1/ 2/41
Cunningham, W.	1/ 2/41
Stevenson, J.	1/ 2/41
Banks, J.	1/ 2/41
Latt, E. L. B. (Lt. late	
Dorset R.)	1/ 2/41
Murray, J. B., M.M.	1/ 2/41
Graham, G., (Lt. late A. & S.H.)	1/ 2/41
Smith, J.	1/ 2/41
White, M. A.	1/ 2/41
Dalton, J.	1/ 2/41
Forsyth, W. F.	1/ 2/41
Hamilton, E.	1/ 2/41
Warren, J. D. N. (Lt. late	
C. Gds.)	1/ 2/41
Campbell, J.	1/ 2/41
McDermid, N.	10/ 7/41

2nd Lieutenants

Cook, H.	1/ 2/41
Wilkie, R. (2/Lt. late	
Camerons)	1/ 2/41
Donald, P. C.	1/ 2/41
Craig, A. F.	1/ 2/41
Greenlees, R. C.	1/ 2/41
McDonald, J. (Lt. late	
London R.)	1/ 2/41
Thomson, J. M.	1/ 2/41
McGeoch, D.	1/ 2/41
Howat, G. R.	1/ 2/41
McKay, J. R.	1/ 2/41
Manwell, J.	1/ 2/41
Adger, J.	1/ 2/41
Young, W. G. (2/Lt. late T.A.)	1/ 2/41

2nd Lieutenants — contd.

Lochrie, A. P., (2/Lt. late	
H.L.I.)	1/ 2/41
McQueen, H.	1/ 2/41
Wallace, C. G., M.M.	1/ 2/41
Hayes, G.	1/ 2/41
Swanson, E.	1/ 2/41
Morrison, D. (Lt. late	
R.S. Fus.)	1/ 2/41
Rennie, J.	1/ 2/41
Millar, J.	1/ 2/41
Gowan, A. G.	1/ 2/41
Smith, C. L.	1/ 2/41
Kerr, A. K.	1/ 2/41
Mundell, J.	1/ 2/41
Sanderson, J. C., D.C.M.	1/ 2/41
Murray, J. St. C. (2/Lt.	
late A. & S.H.)	1/ 2/41
Russell, G.	1/ 2/41
Rourke, H.	1/ 2/41
Berry, A. (Lt. late A. & S.H.)	1/ 2/41

Adjutant & Quarter-Master

Medical Officer

Watt, Maj. J. C., (2/Lt. late	
R.F.C.)	1/ 2/41

3rd RENFREWSHIRE BATTALION

Lt.-Colonel
Hardie, W. B., M.C. (Capt. late T.A.)	1/ 2/41

Majors
Dawson, W. B., M.B.E., M.C., (Maj. late R.E.)	1/ 2/41
MacNaughton, D., M.C., (Capt. late T.A.)	1/ 2/41
Greenshields, D. Mck., D.S.O. (Capt. late T.A.)	1/ 2/41
Whinster, H. N., (Lt. late T.A.)	1/ 2/41
Barrie, J. (Capt. late H.L.I.)	1/ 2/41
Kirkwood, J. R. N., D.S.O., (Maj. late R.E.)	31/ 5/41
Helme, G. S., T.D., (Maj. late R.A.)	1/ 6/41
Pettigrew, P., M.M.	2/ 6/41

Captains
Paine, J. W. R. (Capt. late T.A.)	1/ 2/41
Doyle, J. P. (Paymr. Lt. late R.N.R.)	1/ 2/41
Meikle, L. A. (Capt. late Manch. R.)	1/ 2/41
Sorley, D., M.C. (Capt. late T.A.)	1/ 2/41
Balfour-Ritchie, A. A., (Lt. late T.A.)	1/ 2/41
Gordon, J.	1/ 2/41
Watson, A. (Lt. late T.A.)	1/ 2/41
Jamieson, A. F. D.	2/ 6/41

Lieutenants
Macfarlane, J. W.	1/ 2/41
Forster, J. P.	1/ 2/41
Jack, J. (Capt. late Essex R.)	1/ 2/41
Gartshore, J. W.	1/ 2/41
Small, G. H.	1/ 2/41
Thomson, R.	1/ 2/41

Lieutenants - contd.
Peacock, W. (Lt. late R. Scots.)	1/ 2/4
Clark, J.	1/ 2/4
Patterson, T. R.	1/ 2/4
Murray, G. A. (Capt. late Cameronians)	1/ 2/4
Fraser, T. (2/Lt. late R.A.F.)	1/ 2/41
Morton, W. H. (Lt. late R.E.)	1/ 2/4
Stoddart, J. T.	1/ 2/4
Booth, C. H.	1/ 2/4
Everatt, P. G. (2/Lt. late W. York R.)	1/ 2/4
Petrie, C. (Lt. late R. Lan. R.)	1/ 2/41
O'Neill, W.	1/ 2/4
Morren, A. G.	1/ 2/4
Geldart, T. H.	1/ 2/41
McGlashan, J. A. (Lt.-Col. late H.L.I.)	1/ 2/41
Shearer, T., M.C., (Capt. late A. & S.H.)	1/ 2/4
Broomfield, T. (Capt. late K.O.S.B.)	1/ 2/41
Ferguson, T.	1/ 2/41
Smith, A. R.	1/ 2/41
Carswell, R. A. (F/O late R.F.C.)	1/ 2/4
Wright, P. L. W.	1/ 2/4
Watson, D. (Capt. late A. & S.H.)	1/ 2/4
Fleming, J. H.	1/ 2/41
Templeton, W. (Lt. late R.S. Fus.)	1/ 2/4
Sayer, H. A. E. (2/Lt. late R. Fus.)	1/ 2/4
Fitzpatrick, H. J. (Capt. late T.A.)	1/ 2/41
Wotherspoon, J. A., M.B.E., (Maj. late R.E.)	1/ 2/41
Maclean, A., D.C.M.	26/ 6/4

3rd Renfrewshire Battalion - contd.

2nd Lieutenants
Cameron, J. F. (Lt. late
  Cameronian)   1/ 2/41
Macbroom, R.   1/ 2/41
Holmes, W. K. (Lt. late
  R.F.A.)   1/ 2/41
Craig, J.   1/ 2/41
Logan, J., M.M.   1/ 2/41
Maclachlan, D. C.   1/ 2/41
Connell, J. (2/Lt. late
  A. & S.H.)   1/ 2/41
Galbraith, T.   1/ 2/41
Clark, W. P.   1/ 2/41
Watson, J.   1/ 2/41
Mayer, A. J. (Maj. late H.L.I.)   1/ 2/41
Campbell, C. (Capt. late
  A. & S.H.)   1/ 2/41
Fletcher, A. (Lt. late H.L.I.)   1/ 2/41
Gillespie, J. K.   1/ 2/41
Dove, J.   1/ 2/41
Snodgrass, H. J. (Capt. late
  T.A.)   1/ 2/41
Bussell, D. F. J.   1/ 2/41
Banks, D. K.   1/ 2/41
Tait, A. L.   1/ 2/41
Pullar, W. A. (Lt. late
  Seaforth)   1/ 2/41
Blair, R. H. (Lt. late
  Gordons)   1/ 2/41
Grant, T.   1/ 2/41
Gemmell, W. (Lt. late R.E.)   1/ 2/41
Lawson, A. (2/Lt. late
  Black Watch)   1/ 2/41
Hull, A. G. (Lt. late
  Cameronians)   1/ 2/41
McCandlish, W. K.   1/ 2/41
Wilson, J. (Lt. late T.A.)   1/ 2/41
McDonald, J. S. (Capt. late
  R.A.F.)   1/ 2/41
Izett, H. S. (Lt. late
  R.A.F.)   1/ 2/41
Wilson, F. R. (Capt. late
  Black Watch)   1/ 2/41
Stephen, R. (Lt. late T.A.
  Res.)   1/ 2/41

2nd Lieutenants - contd.
Kater, A.   1/ 7/41
Skinner, A.   1/ 7/41
Mushot, D.   1/ 7/41
Hay, W.   1/ 7/41

Adjutant & Quarter-Master

Medical Officer
Black, Maj. J. B., M.C.,
  (Capt. late R.T.C.)   1/ 2/41

GLASGOW AREA - contd.

NO. 5 ZONE (RENFREW & BUTE) - contd.

4th RENFREWSHIRE BATTALION

Lt.-Colonel
Heys, F. W., M.C., T.D.,
(Maj. late T.A. Res.) — 1/ 2/41

Majors
McCallum, H. G. (Capt. late T.A.) — 1/ 2/41
Hirst, C. J., M.C., T.D., (Maj.
late T.A.) — 6/ 6/41
Gillespie, J. — 6/ 6/41
Brown, J. — 6/ 6/41
Peacock, W. S. (Capt. late R.A.) — 6/ 6/41
Kendrick, V. J. M. (Capt. late
Ind. Army) — 6/ 6/41
Haddow, W. B., (Maj. late
R.S. Fus.) — 6/ 6/41

Captains
Thomson, M. — 1/ 2/41
Hammond, F. (Lt. late
Cheshire R.) — 6/ 6/41
Caldwell, J. (Lt. late
M.G. Corps) — 7/ 6/41
Hannah, D. H. (Lt. late
A. & S.H.) — 7/ 6/41
Cowan, I. C., D.S.O., M.C.,
(Maj. late T.A. Res.) — 7/ 6/41
Coats, I. P. (Lt. Cmdr.
late R.N.) — 7/ 6/41

Lieutenants
Partridge, E. (Capt. late
H.L.I.) — 1/ 2/41
Laird, G., M.M. — 1/ 2/41
Brown, J. B. — 1/ 2/41
Steele, J. S. (2/Lt. late R.E.) — 1/ 2/41
Macbryde, A., M.M. (Maj.
late A. & S.H.) — 1/ 2/41
Goudie, J. M. — 1/ 2/41
Cropper, J. A. — 1/ 2/41
Elias, W. G., M.C. (Lt.
late M.G. Corps) — 1/ 2/41
Fotheringham, J. R. — 1/ 2/41
Lindsay, J. (Lt. late A. & S.H.) — 1/ 2/41
Donaldson, A. — 1/ 2/41
Lyon, I. M. — 6/ 6/41
Kerr, R. R. — 6/ 6/41
Wilson, W. A. (Capt. late
Rifle Bde.) — 6/ 6/41

Lieutenants - contd.
Malcolm, R. H. — 6/ 6/41
McKie, W. T., M.C., (Capt.
late Camerons) — 6/ 6/41
Murray, W., D.C.M., M.M. — 6/ 6/41
Surtees, V. N. F. (Lt. late
K.O.S.B.) — 6/ 6/41
Fraser, W. (2/Lt. late R.E.) — 6/ 6/41
Collyer, H. J. (Lt. late
S. Stafford R.) — 6/ 6/41
Munro, J. McK. (Capt. late T.A.) — 6/ 6/41
Chisholm, T. — 6/ 6/41
Carpenter, T. D. — 7/ 6/41
Fraser, H. C. — 1/ 7/41
Parry, W. — 1/ 7/41
Pinkerton, J. — 1/ 7/41
McLaren, J. L. — 13/ 7/41
Hamilton, W. — 13/ 7/41
Neilson, R. — 13/ 7/41

2nd Lieutenants
Lorains, J. P., M.C. (Lt.
late R.E.) — 1/ 2/41
Stewart, J. — 1/ 2/41
Nicholson, L. G. — 1/ 2/41
Read, W. M. — 1/ 2/41
Hewson, W. N. (2/Lt. late T.A.) — 6/ 6/41
Whiteford, J. M. — 6/ 6/41
Eaglesim A. — 6/ 6/41
Scott, R. L. C. — 6/ 6/41
Abercrombie, W. D. — 6/ 6/41
Brown, J. — 6/ 6/41
Pringle, J. H. (Lt. late
A. & S.H.) — 6/ 6/41
Wilson, J. — 17/ 6/41
Cameron, J. — 25/ 6/41

Adjutant & Quarter-Master
Swan, Capt. (actg. 19/5/41)
R., A. & S.H. — 19/ 5/41

Medical Officers
Brown, Maj. D. McL. (Capt.
late R.F.A.) — 1/ 2/41
Cumming, Maj. A., M.B. — 21/ 7/41
Drever, Capt. G. D., M.B.,
(Capt. late Ind. Army) — 21/ 7/41

GLASGOW AREA — contd.

NO. 6 ZONE (DUMFRIES)

mmander

May, Col., Sir Reginald S. K.C.B.
K.B.E., C.M.G., D.S.O., (Gen.
ret. pay) (Res. of Off.)   1/ 2/41

rritorial Army Association }
  administering

Dumfries T.A. Association
Drill Hall, Dumfries

1st DUMFRIESSHIRE BATTALION

Lt.-Colonel

rdwood, Sir Eric S.,
.B.E., C.B., C.M.G., (Maj.-
en. ret. pay) Res. of Off.)
(Col. Cameronians)   1/ 2/41

Majors

alston, D., M.C., T.D. (Maj.
late T.A.)   1/ 2/41
ere, R. J. H. H., (Lt.-Col.
late R.A.F.)   1/ 2/41
ell-Irving, J., (Maj. late
T.A.)   23/ 4/41
acdonald, W. M. B. (Lt. late
Can. Mil. Forces)   23/ 4/41
lliot, W. D., (Capt. late
Camerons)   23/ 4/41

Captains

cMillar, W. S., (Capt. late
R. Signals)   1/ 2/41
mith, V. W., M.C., V.D., (Capt.
late T.A.)   1/ 2/41
eadman, J. J., D.S.O., (Lt.-
Col. late the Greys)   1/ 2/41
ordon, S., M.C., (Maj. late
Ind. Med. Serv.)   1/ 2/41

Lieutenants

Henderson, J. R., M.C., (Capt.
late R. Scots)   1/ 2/41
Hastie, H. J. A.   1/ 2/41
Rae, W. J.   1/ 2/41
Corlett, A. Q.   1/ 2/41
Moffat, A. G.   23/ 4/41
Bailey, R. L., M.C.   10/ 7/41
Todd, H. B., M.C., M.M.
(Lt. late R.S. Fus.)   10/ 7/41

2nd Lieutenant

Graham, T. C., D.C.M.   1/ 2/41

Adjutant & Quarter-Master

Medical Officer

2nd DUMFRIESSHIRE BATTALION

Lt.-Colonel

Somerville, H., M.C., (Capt. late
Serv. Bn. Monch. R.)   1/ 2/41

Majors

Tomeny, G. A., (Capt. late H.L.I.) 1/ 2/41
Dabbs, J. G. (Capt. late T.A.)   1/ 2/41
Baldwin, A. W., (Capt. late T.A.)   1/ 2/41
Spittal, J., (Capt. late T.A.)   1/ 2/41

Captains

Hunt, N. H.,   1/ 2/41
Dobie, W. G. M., (Lt. late T.A.)   1/ 2/41
Macmurdo, J. N., (Maj. late
T.A.)   1/ 2/41

Lieutenants

Bell, R.   1/ 2/41
McCall, J. H., D.C.M.   1/ 2/41
Stokes, G. D. C., (Capt. late
R.A.)   1/ 2/41
Johnston, T.   1/ 2/41
Kirk, R. G. J., (F/Lt. late
R.A.F.)   1/ 2/41
Greenhill, F. A.   1/ 2/41
Reid, D. H.   1/ 2/41
Brown, J. H.   1/ 2/41
Salvesen, G. A., (Capt. late
T.A.)   1/ 2/41
Johnstone, I. M.   1/ 2/41
Readman, J. F. A., M.C., (Maj.
late R.E.)   1/ 2/41
Dinwiddie, J. S.   1/ 2/41
Ross, D. G., (2/Lt. late M.G.
Corps.)   1/ 2/41
Douglas-Menzies, N. E., (Lt.
late R.A.)   1/ 2/41
Harper, J. M.,   1/ 2/41
Rogers, D. B.   1/ 2/41
Crawford, J. C.   1/ 2/41

Lieutenants - contd.

Ricalton, W.   1/ 2/41
Renton, J., (Lt. late
Camerons)   1/ 2/41
Wallace, Q., (2/Lt. late R.A.)   1/ 2/41
Will, W. J., M.M.   1/ 2/41
Brown, W. J. MacK. (Lt. late
Gordons.)   1/ 2/41

2nd Lieutenants

Muir, W. G.,   1/ 2/41
Muir, A.   1/ 2/41
Scott, W. F. C.   1/ 2/41
Templeton, W.   1/ 2/41
Bell, J.   1/ 2/41
Parker, G.   1/ 2/41
Burnett, T. R.   1/ 2/41
McQueen, R. G.   1/ 2/41
Aitken, J.   1/ 2/41
Muir, S.   1/ 2/41
Garven, A. B.,(Lt. late
R.S. Fus.)   1/ 2/41
Graham, P.   1/ 2/41
Wilson, A.   1/ 2/41
Corrie, T.   1/ 2/41
Tait, S.   1/ 2/41
Byrne, P. J.   1/ 2/41

Adjutant & Quarter-Master

Lindesay, Capt. (actg. 10/3/41)
J. H. C., A. & S.H.   10/ 3/41

Medical Officer

3rd DUMFRIESSHIRE BATTALION		4th DUMFRIESSHIRE BATTALION	

3rd DUMFRIESSHIRE BATTALION

Lt.-Colonel
Steel, J. (Capt. late 2nd L.G.) 1/ 2/41

Majors
Boulter, F. C., M.C. (Capt.
  late R.A.)   1/ 2/41
Dykes, T.   1/ 2/41
Graham, W. F., O.B.E. (Lt.
  late K.O.S.B.)   1/ 2/41
Bell, E. J., T.D. (Maj. late
  T.A.)   1/ 2/41

Captains
Hunter, C. F., D.S.O. (Lt.-Col.
  late K.D.G.)   1/ 2/41
Martin, D. R.   1/ 2/41
Hyslop, M. J. (Lt. late R.S.
  Fus.)   1/ 2/41
Tweedie, G. G. S. (Lt. late
  K.O.S.B.)   1/ 2/41

Lieutenants
Lockhart, A.   1/ 2/41
Irving, A.   1/ 2/41
Dowding, I. A. T.   1/ 2/41
McLean, W. J.   1/ 2/41
Broach, R.   1/ 2/41
Mellour, H.   1/ 2/41
Semple, A. R.   1/ 2/41
Tinning, J. H.   1/ 2/41
Lynch, H. (2/Lt. late R.Signals) 1/ 2/41
Boggis, A. H. G.   1/ 2/41
McGeorge, J. (Maj. late K.O.S.B.)1/ 2/41
Martin, R. (Capt. late
  R. Glos. H.)   1/ 2/41
Willis, E. W.   1/ 2/41
Monro, I. A. S. H. (Capt. Res.
  of Off.)   1/ 2/41
Dickson, J. J. P.   1/ 2/41
Warwick, D. J.   1/ 2/41

2nd Lieutenants
Scott, W. F.   1/ 2/41
Millar, J. G. (Lt. late R.A.F.) 1/ 2/41
Sloggie, J. S.   1/ 2/41
Douglas, R.   1/ 2/41

Adjutant & Quarter-Master

Medical Officer
Thompson, Maj., F. S. C.
  (Lt.-Col. late Ind. Med.
  Serv.)   19/ 6/41

4th DUMFRIESSHIRE BATTALION

Lt.-Colonel
Wilson, A. (Capt. late R.E.)   1/ 2/41

Majors
Macmillan, N.   1/ 2/41
Cowan, J. McI.   1/ 2/41
Bruce, G. S.   23/ 4/41
Niven, W. (Capt. late Ind.
  Army)   23/ 4/41
Mackie, P. S.   23/ 4/41

Captains
Hume, A. D. (Lt. late
  R. Scots.)   22/ 4/41
Sim, A.   23/ 4/41
Dunn, H. R.   23/ 4/41
Cowan, J.   23/ 4/41
Smith, J. W. T.   23/ 4/41

Lieutenants
Hunter, J. H.   1/ 2/41
Crosbie, R. D.   1/ 2/41
Maclachlan, R.   1/ 2/41
Young, J. McC.   1/ 2/41
Miller, A.   1/ 2/41
Little, J. E.   1/ 2/41
Barron, J. V. E. (Lt. late
  Gordons)   1/ 2/41
Hawley, McH. M.   22/ 4/41
Hutchings, A. C.   22/ 4/41
Gordon, J.   22/ 4/41
Ruffell, J. B. D.   22/ 4/41
Kirkpatrick, W.   23/ 4/41
Black, A.   23/ 4/41
Erskine, A.   23/ 4/41

2nd Lieutenants
Orr, R.   1/ 2/41
Thompson, K. W.   1/ 2/41
Barbour, J. M.   22/ 4/41
Currie, D.   22/ 4/41
Muir, J. M. C.   22/ 4/41
Bolton, R., D.C.M.   6/ 6/41
Lennox, W. R. (Capt. late
  A. & S.H.)   30/ 6/41

Adjutant & Quarter-Master

Medical Officer
Edgar, Maj., T. B., M.B.   1/ 2/41

GLASGOW AREA – contd.

NO. 7 ZONE (KIRKCUDBRIGHTSHIRE)

Commander	Pitt–Taylor, Col. <u>Sir</u> Walter W., K.C.B., <u>C.M.G.</u>, <u>D.S.O.</u> (Gen. ret. pay) 1/ 2/41
Second–in–Command	Brown, Lt.–Col., P. W., <u>C.M.G.</u>, D.S.O. (Hon. Brig.–Gen ret.pay) 1/ 2/41
Chief Guide Officer	Mitchell, Capt., J., <u>V.D.</u> (<u>Lt.–</u> <u>Col. late Ind. Army</u>) 1/ 2/41
Liaison Officer	Williams, Capt., F. H. 1/ 2/41
Weapon Training Officer	Cliff–McCulloch, Capt. W. E. (<u>Lt. late S. Gds.</u>) 23/ 6/41
Territorial Army Association administering	County of Kirkudbrightshire T.A. Association
	Drill Hall, Dumfries

1st KIRKCUDBRIGHTSHIRE BATTALION

Lt.–Colonel

MacEwen, M. L., C.B. (<u>Hon. Brig.–Gen. ret. pay</u>)	1/ 2/41

Majors

Villiers–Stuart, W. D., <u>C.B.E.</u>, <u>D.S.O.</u>, (<u>Brig.–Gen. late Ind. Army</u>)	1/ 2/41
Fisher, J. A. (<u>Maj. late K.O.S.B.</u>)	1/ 2/41
Murdoch, A. N. (<u>Capt. late T.A.</u>)	1/ 2/41

Captains

Macleod, R. M., <u>M.C.</u> (<u>Capt. late T.A.</u>)	1/ 2/41
Rainsford–Hannay, F., <u>C.M.G.</u>, <u>D.S.O.</u>, (<u>Col. ret. pay</u>)	1/ 2/41
Allan, A. E., (<u>Lt. late R.F.C.</u>)	1/ 2/41

Lieutenants

Chesney, W. A.	1/ 2/41
Craigie, C. F.	1/ 2/41
Jennings, I. McI.	1/ 2/41
Sinclair, <u>Lord</u>, M. V. O. (<u>Capt. late The Greys</u>)	1/ 2/41
Nelson, J., (<u>2/Lt. ret.</u>)	1/ 2/41
Marsh, F. C.	1/ 2/41
McGregor, J. A., <u>M.C.</u>, <u>M.M.</u> (<u>Lt. late Can. Mil. Forces</u>)	1/ 2/41
Dodd, G. E. (<u>late Can. Mil. Forces</u>)	1/ 2/41

Lieutenants – contd.

Cochrane, D. C. (<u>Lt. late R. Scots.</u>)	1/ 2/41
Williams, G. H.	1/ 2/41
Corrie, A. J. (<u>Lt. T.A. Res.</u>)	1/ 2/41
McCall, A. I.	1/ 2/41
Brown, A. C.	1/ 2/41
Hogg, J. A.	1/ 2/41
Kennedy, <u>Lord</u> (<u>Capt. late T.A.</u>)	1/ 2/41
Warnock, J., <u>M.C.</u> (<u>Capt. late R.E.</u>)	4/ 6/41
Hotenkis, M. H.	17/ 6/41

2nd Lieutenants

McWilliam, W. H.	1/ 2/41
Bryden, W.	1/ 2/41
Clark, J. Y. F.	1/ 2/41
Core, W.	1/ 2/41
Gray, A.	1/ 2/41
Picken, J. (<u>Lt. late T.A.</u>)	1/ 2/41
Milligan, J.	1/ 2/41
Clark, H.	1/ 2/41
Taylor, F. A.	1/ 2/41
Nicholson, D. H. B.	5/ 7/41
Rennie, M.	27/ 7/41

Adjutant & Quarter-Master

Callander, Capt. (<u>actg. 11/3/41</u>) C. Gen. List Inf.	11/ 3/41

Medical Officer

Carmichael, Maj., L. G., M.B.,	1/ 2/41

GLASGOW AREA -- contd.

No. 7'ZONE (KIRKCUDBRIGHTSHIRE) -- contd.

2nd KIRKCUDBRIGHTSHIRE BATTALION

Lt.-Colonel
Morris, T. A. P. (Bt. Lt.-Col.
late H.L.I.)   1/ 2/41

Majors
Oswald, R. A. (Capt. late Ind.
Army)   1/ 2/41
Lake, B. C., D.S.O. (Col.
ret. pay) (Res. of Off.)   1/ 2/41

Captains
Stewart, A. M.   1/ 2/41
Burns-Thomson, J. F. M.
(2/Lt. late R.S. Fus.)   1/ 2/41

Lieutenants
Austin, S. T. W.   1/ 2/41
Barton, P. G., M.C. (Capt.
late R. Fus.)   1/ 2/41
Hanbury, R. F. (Capt. late
T.A.)   1/ 2/41
Haugh, A. St. L. F. (Capt.
late R.S. Fus.)   1/ 2/41
McQueen, J. W. D.   1/ 2/41
Brodie, S. H., M.C. (Capt.
late R.A.)   1/ 2/41
Hutchison, C. G. G. (Lt.-
Col. ret.)   1/ 2/41
Tillotson, P.   1/ 2/41
Kelland, N. S.   1/ 2/41
Rundell, W. W. O. (Maj. late
Scottish H.)   1/ 2/41

56455-3(113)

2nd Lieutenants
Crabb, J. A.   1/ 2/41
Bayetto, R. A.   1/ 2/41
Boyd, T. (Capt. late R.E.)   1/ 2/41
McTurk, T.   1/ 2/41
Mackay, R. W. (Capt. late
K.A. Rif.)   1/ 2/41
Campbell, J. K.   1/ 2/41
McMeekin, T.   1/ 6/41
Dow, D.   15/ 6/41
Nicholson, T. I.   23/ 7/41

Adjutant & Quarter-Master

Medical Officer
Gemmell, Maj. R. G.   1/ 2/41

GLASGOW AREA - contd.

No. 8 ZONE (WIGTOWN)

Commander	Stair, Col. The Earl of, K.T., D.S.O. (Lt.-Col. ret. pay)(Hon. Col. T.A.) 1/ 2/41
Liaison Officer	Nicol, Capt., J. B. 1/ 2/41
Territorial Army Association Administering	County of Wigtown T.A. Association, Drill Hall, Dumfries

---

1st WIGTOWNSHIRE (RHINNS) BATTALION

Lt.-Colonel

Ewing, A.   1/ 2/41

Majors

Rae, D. (Capt. late T.A.)   1/ 2/41
Paton, E. G. (2/Lt. late R.T. Corps)   1/ 2/41
Parker, W. W.   1/ 2/41
Vallance, J. (2/Lt. late T.A.)   1/ 2/41
McIntyre, J. M.   1/ 2/41

Captains

McHarrie, J.   1/ 2/41
Fisher, I.   1/ 2/41
McCracken, T.   1/ 2/41
Wither, J.   1/ 2/41

Lieutenants

Mair, H. K. C.   1/ 2/41
McHaig, D.   1/ 2/41
Stewart, A.   1/ 2/41
Wingate, T.   1/ 2/41
Bailey, H. G. C.   1/ 2/41
Rye, R. W.   1/ 2/41
Wyllie, J. H.   1/ 2/41
Murray, J. H.   1/ 2/41
Shearer, A. J. R. (Capt. late, K.S.L.I.)   1/ 2/41

56455-3(114)

Lieutenants - contd.

McIntyre, J.   1/ 2/41
Wilson, J.   1/ 2/41
Lamont, R.   1/ 2/41
McCaig, R. Y.   1/ 2/41
Tully, J. P.   1/ 2/41
Hannat, J. M.   1/ 2/41

2nd Lieutenants

Hogg, J.   1/ 2/41
Clark, H. G.   1/ 2/41
McHaffie, T. A.   1/ 2/41
Douglas, W. T.   1/ 2/41
Murray, A.   1/ 2/41
Stevenson, R.   1/ 2/41
Findlay, W.   1/ 2/41
Vallance, R.   1/ 2/41
Dunlop, G.   1/ 2/41
Muir, J.   1/ 2/41
Cochran, J.   1/ 2/41
McMurray, D.   1/ 2/41

Adjutant & Quarter-Master

Medical Officer

Anderson, Maj., F. A., M.C., M.B., (Capt. late R.A.M.C.)   1/ 2/41

2nd WIGTOWNSHIRE (MACHERS) BATTALION

		2nd Lieutenants	
Lt.-Colonel		Mackenzie, R. W.	1/ 2/41
Merrilees, A.	1/ 2/41	Owen, R.	1/ 2/41
		McGeoch, J. A.	1/ 2/41
		Paterson, J.	1/ 2/41
		McClymont, D.	1/ 2/41
		Tyne, A. T.	1/ 2/41
		McCaull, D. (Lt. late R.A.F.)	1/ 2/41
		Hannay, J.	1/ 2/41
Majors		Maclean, A.	1/ 2/41
McNeill, L. (2/Lt. late		Roy, D. C. B.	1/ 2/41
K.O.S.B.)	1/ 2/41	Nicholson, J.	1/ 2/41
McCaig, W. H.	1/ 2/41	Brown, W. A.	1/ 2/41
Hannay, W.	1/ 2/41	Christie, J. A.	1/ 2/41
Wyllie, J. T. (Capt. late		Allan, R.	1/ 2/41
T.A.)	1/ 2/41	Coid, C.	1/ 2/41
Douglas, R., M.M.	1/ 2/41	Stevenson, J. A., M.M.	1/ 2/41
		McGowan, W.	1/ 2/41
		Millar, J.	1/ 2/41
		Christison, C.	1/ 2/41

Captains		
Fletcher, P. H. (Lt. late		
T.A.)	1/ 2/41	
Walker, A. N. (Lt. late		
T.A.)	1/ 2/41	**Adjutant & Quarter-Master**

Lieutenants		**Medical Officer**	
Stewart, W. A.	1/ 2/41	Brown, Maj. G.	1/ 2/41
Lees, J. C. (Lt. late			
R.A.F.)	1/ 2/41		
McCreath, H. M. (Capt.			
late Seaforth)	1/ 2/41		

56455-3(115)

GLASGOW AREA — contd.
NO.9 ZONE (SOUTH ARGYLL)

Commander	Speed, Col. D. C. L., O.B.E. (Capt. late K.R.R.C.) 1/ 2/41
Second-in-Command	Hardie, Lt.-Col. J. S. (Capt. late T.A.) 1/ 2/41
Intelligence Officer	Galbraith, Capt., J. (Capt. late A. & S.H.) 7/ 5/41
Liaison Officer	Lamont, Capt., J. W. F., C.B., C.M.G., D.S.O., (Hon. Brig.-Gen. ret. pay) 1/ 2/41
Chief Guide	Macfaden, Capt., M. (Maj. ret.) 1/ 2/41
Territorial Army Association Administering }	Argyll T.A. Association, The Drill Hall, Hanover Street, Dunoon.

1st ARGYLL (SOUTH ARGYLL) BATTALION

Colonel
Speed, D. C. L., O.B.E. (Capt. late K.R.R.C.)   1/ 2/41

Majors
Burn, J. R. P. (Capt. late Seaforth)   1/ 2/41
Galbraith, D.   1/ 2/41
Blaine, G., M.C. (Capt. late T.A.)   1/ 2/41
Stobart, F. E. (Capt. late 18th H.)   17/ 6/41

Captains
Tatton, G.   1/ 2/41
Glen, T. (Lt. late R.A.)   1/ 2/41
Stuart, D. N. (Lt. late R.A.)   1/ 2/41

Lieutenants
de Chair, Sir Dudley, K.C.B., K.C.M.G., M.V.O., D.S.O. (Admiral ret.)   1/ 2/41
Paterson, G. S.   1/ 2/41
Macgilp, C. A.   1/ 2/41
Campbell-Blair, J. (Capt. late R. North'd. Fus.)   1/ 2/41
Mackay, A.   1/ 2/41
Watson, D., M.M. (2/Lt. late Black Watch)   1/ 2/41
Laing, J. S. (2/Lt. late R. W. Fus.) 1/ 2/41
Cranston, J. H.   1/ 2/41
MacNab, A.   1/ 2/41
Sandeman, C. S. (Maj. late R.A.M.C.)   1/ 2/41
Cameron, A. D.   1/ 2/41
Robertson, G. N. (Capt. late Gordons)   1/ 2/41
Warlow, P. L. (Capt. late T.A.) 1/ 2/41
Parsons, L. T.   1/ 2/41

Lieutenants — contd.
Turnbull, J. W. (Lt. late T.A.) 1/ 2/41
Smith, G. C. (Maj. late R.S. Fus.)   1/ 2/41
Roberts, F. R., M.C. (Capt. late R. Fus.)   1/ 2/41

2nd Lieutenants
Clark, R.   1/ 2/41
Sherwin, F. G. J.   1/ 2/41
Jackson, D.   1/ 2/41
McLean, D. G. (Capt. late Gordons)   1/ 2/41
Vair-Turnbull, I.   1/ 2/41
Stewart, A. D.   1/ 2/41
Macpherson, G.   1/ 2/41
Armour, J. (Lt. late A. & S.H.)   20/ 6/41
Lorimer, J., V.D.   28/ 6/41
Macpherson, A. M.   28/ 6/41
Annan, J. McC.   11/ 7/41
McNeill, W. N. (Lt. late R. Ir. Rif.)   13/ 8/41
Hamilton, J. McQ. (Lt. late R.N.R.)   13/ 8/41

Adjutant & Quarter-Master
Kinloch, Capt. (actg. 8/5/41) W., Gen. List Inf.   8/ 5/41

Medical Officer
Mackenzie, Maj. C. C., M.B.,   1/ 2/41

Territorial Army Association administering	Orkney T.A. Association, Junction Road, Kirkwall, Orkney.

1st ORKNEY BATTALION

2nd ORKNEY BATTALION

Lt.-Colonel
Brown, G., M.B.E.   1/ 2/41

Majors
Scarth, R. (2/Lt. late T.A.)   1/ 2/41
Bruce, J. (Lt. late Seaforth)   1/ 2/41
Baillie, J.   1/ 2/41

Captains
Buchanan, F. (Lt.-Col. late R.A.)   1/ 2/41

Lieutenants
Hourston, C.   1/ 2/41
Towers, T. C., M.M.   1/ 2/41
Hepburn, D. K.   1/ 2/41
Comloquey, J. H.   1/ 2/41
Ritch, W.   1/ 2/41
Scott, W. (2/Lt. late R.G.A.)   1/ 2/41
Eunson, D.   1/ 2/41
Stove, R. D.   1/ 2/41
Laughton, D. J., M.M.   1/ 2/41
Gorie, J. S.   1/ 2/41
Gray, J. E.   12/ 8/41

2nd Lieutenants
Cromerty, R., D.C.M.   1/ 2/41
Spence, R. S.   1/ 2/41
Bichan, R., M.M.   1/ 2/41
Scott, J.   1/ 2/41
Dickson, J. W. (Capt. late R. Scots)   1/ 2/41
Scott, J. T. W.   1/ 2/41
Drever, W.   1/ 2/41
Garrioch, W. T.   1/ 2/41

Adjutant & Quarter-Master
Shearer, Capt. (actg. 1/ 2/41) R. E., T.A.   1/ 2/41

Medical Officer
Sinclair, Maj., W. A. (2/Lt. late Seaforth)   1/ 2/41

Territorial Army Association
  administering   }

Zetland T.A. Association,
  Lerwick.

1st ZETLAND BATTALION

Lt.-Colonel
Nicolson, Sir Arthur J. F. W.,
  Bt. (Lt. late R.N.V.R.)   1/ 2/41

2nd Lieutenants – contd.	
Leask, O.	1/ 2/41
Anderson, R. G.	1/ 2/41
Gellatly, J. S.	1/ 2/41
Gair, G.	1/ 2/41
Tait, E. S. R.	1/ 2/41
Johnson, J. C.	1/ 2/41
Smith, A.	1/ 2/41
Goudie, J.	1/ 2/41
Tait, W.	1/ 2/41
Leslie, G. W. B.	1/ 2/41
Millar, A. S.	1/ 2/41
Cruikshank, D. B.	1/ 2/41
Priest, A., M.M.	1/ 2/41
Sandison, I. E. M.	1/ 2/41
Clark, P.	1/ 2/41
Saxby, H. D.	1/ 2/41
Smith, W. A.	1/ 2/41
Garriock, W. J.	1/ 2/41
Todd, M. B.	29/ 7/41

Captains
Irvine, A.	1/ 2/41
Arthur, T. H. (2/Lt. late R. Scots)	1/ 2/41
Laurenson, P. B.	1/ 2/41
Tait, R. W.	1/ 2/41
Sandison, C. G. D.	1/ 2/41

Lieutenants
Johnson, J. T. A.	1/ 2/41
Lyon, A. D.	1/ 2/41
Bell, R. T.	1/ 2/41

Adjutant & Quarter-Master
Campbell, Capt. (actg. 1/2/41)
  G. W. Black Watch.   1/ 2/41

2nd Lieutenants
Thomson, H.	1/ 2/41
Irvine, J.	1/ 2/41
Leask, J. B.	1/ 2/41
Hay, J. J.	1/ 2/41
Sandison, D. H.	1/ 2/41
Pole, J. G. G.	1/ 2/41
Johnson, P. F.	1/ 2/41
Reid, A. K.	1/ 2/41
Tulloch, J. W.	1/ 2/41
Arthurson, J. L.	1/ 2/41

Medical Officer

DEATHS

Lieutenant-Colonel

Boyle, C. A., C.I.E., D.S.O., 1st Ayrshire Battalion (Col. ret.
Ind. Army)

Major

Simson, H. J., M.C., 3rd Aberdeenshire (South and Kincardineshire)
Battalion (Col. ret. pay) (Res. of Off.)

Captain

Heathcote, W., 7th Fifeshire Battalion (Capt. late M.G. Corps)

xi

xiii

Lightning Source UK Ltd.
Milton Keynes UK
UKOW06f2357200716

278899UK00020B/625/P